**Cambridge Elements** ≡

Elements in Soviet and Post-Soviet History
edited by
Mark Edele
*University of Melbourne*
Rebecca Friedman
*Florida International University*

# DECOLONIZING RUSSIA?

## *Disentangling Debates*

Adam Lenton
*Wake Forest University*

and co-authors

**CAMBRIDGE**
UNIVERSITY PRESS

Shaftesbury Road, Cambridge CB2 8EA, United Kingdom

One Liberty Plaza, 20th Floor, New York, NY 10006, USA

477 Williamstown Road, Port Melbourne, VIC 3207, Australia

314–321, 3rd Floor, Plot 3, Splendor Forum, Jasola District Centre,
New Delhi – 110025, India

103 Penang Road, #05–06/07, Visioncrest Commercial, Singapore 238467

Cambridge University Press is part of Cambridge University Press & Assessment,
a department of the University of Cambridge.

We share the University's mission to contribute to society through the pursuit of
education, learning and research at the highest international levels of excellence.

www.cambridge.org
Information on this title: www.cambridge.org/9781009664745

DOI: 10.1017/9781009664738



When citing this work, please include a reference to the DOI 10.1017/9781009664738

First published 2025

*A catalogue record for this publication is available from the British Library*

ISBN 978-1-009-66474-5 Hardback
ISBN 978-1-009-66478-3 Paperback
ISSN 2753-5290 (online)
ISSN 2753-5282 (print)

Cambridge University Press & Assessment has no responsibility for the persistence
or accuracy of URLs for external or third-party internet websites referred to in this
publication and does not guarantee that any content on such websites is, or will
remain, accurate or appropriate.

For EU product safety concerns, contact us at Calle de José Abascal, 56, 1°, 28003
Madrid, Spain, or email eugpsr@cambridge.org

# Decolonizing Russia?

## Disentangling Debates

Elements in Soviet and Post-Soviet History

DOI: 10.1017/9781009664738
First published online: April 2025

Adam Lenton et al.
*Wake Forest University*

and co-authors

**Author for correspondence:** Adam Lenton, lentona@wfu.edu

**Abstract:** Russia's full-scale invasion of Ukraine in February 2022 radically changed the way many viewed the nature of the Russian state. The centrality of resentment and imperial nostalgia in Russian narratives led many to argue that Russian imperialism was a key force behind the invasion. By extension, this led to the idea that decolonization – largely in scholarship, but also among some policy circles – offered a way of better understanding Russia in this new context. To this end, this Element examines the debates over decolonization in the Russian case. It begins by contextualizing these debates through an examination of Russia's historical development as an empire. It then identifies and disentangles three key focal points: decolonization as domestic Russian politics, the transnational politics of decolonization, and decolonization as a scholarly endeavor. By doing so, this Element shows where decolonization has merit, but also where it is contested or limited.

**Keywords:** Russia, empire, history, politics, identity



ISBNs: 9781009664745 (HB), 9781009664783 (PB), 9781009664738 (OC)
ISSNs: 2753-5290 (online), 2753-5282 (print)

# **Contents**


Introduction                                                                        1

1  Identity and Empire in Russian History                         8

2  The Soviet Rule: Decolonial in Form, Colonial in Content?  22

3  Post-Socialist Transition: Decolonization
   and Recolonization                                                          36

4  Decolonization and Its International Dimension          52

5  Decolonization as Scholarship                                       64

   Conclusion                                                                      76

## Introduction

Russia's invasion of Ukraine on February 24, 2022 was framed by President Vladimir Putin as a rightful reclaiming of territories and people considered historically Russian. The justification for the war mixed various arguments, including Russia's strategic interests, defense of ethnic Russians in Donetsk and Luhansk regions, and Crimea's religious significance in Russian history. These justifications undermine Ukraine's sovereignty, framing Ukrainians as part of the Russian nation or questioning Ukraine's legitimacy as an independent state. Many of these arguments echo imperialist ideals, with Putin even praising historical expansionist policies to "return and consolidate" supposed Russian territories, drawing parallels to the ambitions of past Russian emperors like Peter the Great.[1]

The war has relaunched debates about Russia as an empire, a term that, in today's political language, is seen as a negative label that describes a state as questioning the legitimacy and authenticity of another polity. Asserting that Russia is an empire closely correlates to the increasingly prominent question of "decolonizing" it, be it in the sense of changing the way external observers look at it, the way the Russian society and the regime should rethink their national identity, or in a more radical sense of collapsing the Russian state. One of the most striking images from this latter interpretation is a map by the Forum of Free Nations of Post-Russia showing about forty "independent and free states," replete with flags and whose neatly arranged borders are seen to replace the contemporary Russian Federation in its entirety. The map's message is clear: that these territories are latent states-in-waiting, and by extension that there are political communities in whose name these states are to be governed.[2]

This message, however, belies a more complex picture. Some of the territories represented appear to possess credible claims to statehood, whether by virtue of already existing as administrative regions with some degree of autonomy, or through recent experience of regionalist or separatist movements. Yet others appear phantom-like, such as the "Zales'e Federation," a rump agglomeration comprising of much of central Russia and Moscow.

This picture is further complicated when considering the peoples living in these territories. In some, there is little evidence that any distinct political

---

[1] Vladimir Putin, "Vstrecha s molodymi predprinimateliami, inzhenerami i uchenymi," Kremlin.ru, June 9, 2022, https://kremlin.ru/events/president/news/68606. Also available at: "Hailing Peter the Great, Putin Draws Parallel with Mission to 'Return' Russian Lands," *Reuters*, June 9, 2022, https://www.reuters.com/world/europe/hailing-peter-great-putin-draws-parallel-with-mission-return-russian-lands-2022-06-09/.

[2] "A New Architecture for Northern Eurasia: The Sixth Free Nations of Post-Russia Forum," Hudson Institute, April 25, 2023, www.hudson.org/events/new-architecture-northern-eurasia-sixth-free-nations-post-russia-forum.

community exists – indeed, one of the Forum representatives, discussing their region, admitted that "there's no demand of the local population to be independent."[3] Meanwhile, others are inhabited by distinct communities with varying degrees of historical grievances against Moscow, notably in the North Caucasus, the Volga region, and Siberia. Even in these cases, however, there are sizeable minority groups nested *within* these territories – most often ethnic Russians but occasionally other ethnic groups and Indigenous peoples – adding a further layer of complexity to the question of who comprises the political community of these territories. These claims are at times overlapping, with emphasis on differing historical periods as well as divergent cultural realities and memories.

Before delving into the different components of a discussion on Russia as an empire, one needs to look briefly at the multiplicity of terms used: colonialism, post-colonialism, (de)coloniality, empire, imperialism – a conceptual multiplicity that greatly contributes to obscuring the debate.

## Contested Terminologies

Although expansion and conquest of territories has been present throughout human history, the term *colonization* refers specifically to the era from the late fifteenth century until the mid twentieth century, during which states – primarily European but not exclusively – engaged in expansion of their territories to acquire raw materials, cheap labor, rare products, and enlarge their markets. The regime that established practices of political control over another region, occupying it with settlers and exploiting it economically is *colonialism*. Experiences of colonialism in different parts of the world have diverged, depending on the period, length, and forms of colonial dominance. Among common features is appropriation of land and resources, legitimized through the dehumanization of their owners through racialization, orientalization, and exoticization.

*Decolonization* is the act of "unmaking" colonialism through the return of the control over land and resources to the original owners, granting them political rights, and cultural emancipation; that is, lifting of pejorative connotations, imagery, cultural artifacts that continue to reinforce an unequal power balance between the colonizers and the colonized. *Post(-)colonialism* is used to describe the political and cultural struggles of societies that experienced the transition from political dependence to sovereignty. Although the national liberation movements of the post-World War II era brought formal colonization to an end in many parts of the world (post-colonialism), Indigenous peoples still live

---

[3] Author's own observations. We do not provide names, dates, or places to protect the safety of the authors.

in settler-colonial states, and there are ongoing struggles to reclaim control of traditional territories (postcolonialism).[4] Moreover, many of the now-independent regions undergo forms of *neocolonialism* by becoming sources of cheap labor and raw materials to the advantage of the former colonizers, without direct political subjugation.

*Postcolonial theory* refers to the critical academic study that is primarily concerned "with accounting for the political, aesthetic, economic, historical, and social impact of European colonial rule around the world in the 18th through the 20th century."[5] To speak about the "colonial matrix of power" that has been persistent even after the global decolonial movement of the 1950s–1960s, scholars use the term *coloniality*. Developed first by the Latin American school of thought and associated with scholars such as Walter Mignolo, Aníbal Quijano, and Arturo Escobar, coloniality refers to the continuous exploitation of the world and its resources by European systems of domination.[6] An important feature of coloniality is that it makes capitalism, nationalism, and modernity appear universal and inevitable. Fighting against it, *decoloniality*, in the words of Catherine Walsh, "seeks to make visible, open up, and advance radically distinct perspectives and positionalities that displace Western rationality as the only framework and possibility of existence, analysis and thought."[7]

While the semantic space of everything related to colonialism and coloniality is broad and contested, another conceptual space, that of *empire/imperialism* adds to the complexity of our discussions. Most definitions of empire acknowledge the centrality of power, as well as the presence of cultural differences between empires' constituent parts. In one definition often used by scholars of international relations, empire is understood as a "relationship, formal or informal, in which one state controls the effective political sovereignty of another political society."[8] Other definitions place greater emphasis on the presence of hierarchical and asymmetric governance models toward different cultural and

---

[4] Post-colonialism (with the hyphen) often refers to the period following colonial rule whereas postcolonialism (without the hyphen) often refers to theoretical literature about this condition.

[5] J. Daniel Elam, "Postcolonial Theory," Oxford Bibliographies, 2019, DOI: 10.1093/OBO/9780190221911-0069.

[6] Aníbal Quijano, "Coloniality and Modernity/Rationality," *Cultural Studies* 21, no. 2–3 (2007): 168–78; Walter D. Mignolo and Arturo Escobar, *Globalization and the Decolonial Option* (Routledge, 2013).

[7] Catherine Walsh, "The Decolonial For: Resurgences, Shifts and Movements," in *On Decoloniality: Concepts, Analytics, Praxis*, ed. Walter Mignolo and Catherine Walsh (Duke University Press, 2018), 17.

[8] Michael W. Doyle, *Empires* (Cornell University Press, 1986), 45.

territorial groups within empires,[9] often referred to in terms of a "core" versus a culturally differentiated "periphery."[10] In scholarly analysis, colonialism is often used synonymously with imperialism, with the latter describing the most aggressive phase of European colonialism in the second half of the nineteenth century.

Empire is also a value-laden term. As Dominic Lieven put it, at times empire "needs not only to be defined in words but also seen, felt and imagined."[11] If empires – like other political entities such as states – need to be imagined (that is, to be understood to exist by individuals), then it suggests that empire is not only an empirical concept but a normative one. Thus, definitions of empire have changed over time, from being viewed favorably by many in the nineteenth century to contemporary use of the term as a way of questioning the legitimacy of a polity.[12] In this Element we focus analytical attention on both aspects of empire: as an existing hierarchical relationship between different territories and peoples, and as a discursive frame that places domestic and international politics in normative terms. As we illustrate, these aspects are at times complementary; at others, in considerable tension with one another.

## Definitions in Tension: The Russian Context

The Russian political context has produced its own concepts used to describe imperial/colonial situations. The Russian language dissociates for instance *osvoenie* (making something one's own) from colonization. *Osvoenie* is employed to describe the conquest of Siberian territories by Muscovy since the sixteenth century and the idea that these territories were "empty" of populations or at least of "civilized" populations. This can be compared with the conquest of Northern America or Australia by Europeans, and with it the myth of a virgin land waiting to be transformed into arable territories with settlers. Although the conquest of Siberian territories entails features of colonization – subjugation of the Indigenous population and extraction of resources – Russian *osvoenie* had also clear specificities compared with that of Western European colonial powers: "the absence of a clear moment of departure, where the home country was

---

[9] Ronald Grigor Suny, "The Empire Strikes Out: Imperial Russia, 'National' Identity, and Theories of Empire," in *A State of Nations: Empire and Nation-Making in the Age of Lenin and Stalin*, ed. Ronald Grigor Suny and Terry Martin (Oxford University Press, 2001), 25; Jane Burbank and Frederick Cooper, *Empires in World History: Power and the Politics of Difference* (Princeton University Press, 2011).

[10] Alexander J. Motyl, "Thinking about Empire," in *After Empire: Multiethnic Societies and Nation-Building: The Soviet Union and the Russian, Ottoman, and Habsburg Empires*, ed. Karen Barkey and Mark von Hagen (Westview Press, 1997), 21.

[11] Dominic Lieven, *In the Shadow of the Gods: The Emperor in World History* (Penguin, 2022), 23.

[12] Suny, "The Empire Strikes Out," 26–27.

abandoned; a much less highly developed ideology of racial difference; and, before the nineteenth century at least, a tendency to cultural hybridity and a tradition of opposition to central state authority."[13]

The terms colony and colonization (*koloniia* and *kolonizatsiia*) are used in Russian to describe a later stage of conquest, toward the south (Transcaucasia and Central Asia), mostly in the nineteenth century. Contrary to *osvoenie*, *kolonizatsiia* clearly referred to the European experience of colonization and the idea that Russia, too, was bringing civilization to the backward East. As stated by Alexander Morrison:

> The nineteenth century saw the development of a fully-fledged colonial ideology in Russia; the terms *koloniya* and *kolonizatsiya* were used frequently and with positive connotations of modernity and agricultural development. Above all, a legal framework was developed which gave Europeans (mainly Russians and Ukrainians) a pre-eminent right to the use and occupation of the land in the Empire's Asiatic territories, at the direct expense of the indigenous populations, who resisted with both words and (in 1916) with deeds. If race was less often invoked as a justification for this than in Africa, Australia or the Americas, religion, "culture" and perceived loyalty to the state were equally effective substitutes.[14]

The terms empire and imperialism (*imperiia* and *imperializm*) have, too, their complex genealogy. Empire was used by the tsarist regime (tsars became "emperors" in 1721 when Peter the Great took the title of "emperor of all Russia") to describe itself (the Russian Empire, *rossiiskaia imperiia*). It is not a coincidence that in Russia, political philosophy refers positively to the notion of empire, seen as producing a specific "civilization," and opposes it to Western European colonialism as simple political and economic oppression.

After the Bolshevik Revolution in 1917, Soviet historiography developed empire and imperialism as negative labels attributed to both pre-revolutionary Russia and the capitalist West, using these terms during the Cold War to condemn US and Western European neocolonial attitudes towards what was called at that time the Third World. These labels stick. In today's Russia, historiography continues to use empire to qualify pre-revolutionary Russia, mostly positively: The Russian Empire, in this view, was constituted mostly through the "voluntary joining" (*dobrovol'noe vkhozhdenie*) of smaller nations – a narrative that obviously obfuscates the historical realities of the conquest, submission, and violence that occurred in many cases.

---

[13] Alexander Morrison, "Russian Settler Colonialism," in *The Routledge Handbook of the History of Settler Colonialism*, ed. Edward Cavanagh and Lorenzo Veracini (Routledge, 2016), 322.

[14] Ibid.

But official language does not project the Russian Federation as an empire: According to the Constitution, Russia is a "multinational people," that is a civic nation composed of Indigenous peoples (as we can see, *nations* and *peoples* are blurry notions too). The concept of Indigeneity is ambivalent in the Russian context, where several definitions of it coexist in tension: Indigenous (*korennye*) as small-numbered nations of Siberia and the Arctic; Indigenous as all non-Russian ethnic groups who have been conquered over time; or Indigenous as all the peoples living on what is now Russia's territory (as opposed to foreigners or newcomers), meaning that in that case, ethnic Russians are Indigenous too, and not settlers.

This ambiguity is also to be found in the existence of a dual terminology to describe belonging to Russia. This multinational people of Russia mentioned in the Constitution is Rossian (*rossiiskii*); that is, citizen of Russia, theoretically all equal in rights, yet the Russian nation (*russkii*) has a status of first among equals: The 2012 Strategy for Nationalities Policy mentions the Russian people as Russia's "historically system-creating core," and the 2020 Constitutional amendments enshrined the "Russian language as the language of the state-constitutive people, part of the multinational union of equal peoples of the Russian Federation."[15]

As we can see, Russian official language does not use the notion of empire to talk about today's Russia. But this is not the case in Russian far-right intellectual circles, which have rehabilitated the idea of Russia as an empire – seen as positive – to describe the supposed autocratic destiny of the Russian regime and its unique civilizational features, often framed as "imperialness" (*imperskost'*). Some use imperialness to advocate for the territorial conquest of Ukraine (also displayed is the notion of Novorossiya, an eighteenth-century term describing what is now eastern and southern Ukraine, at that time territories conquered by Catherine the Great from the Ottoman Empire), while others deploy it without calling for territorial enlargement.

Another aspect of the Soviet tradition that has been updated by Russian official language is to qualify the Western world as imperialist or (neo)colonial. Amid worsening relations with the West, this rhetoric resurfaces in Kremlin discourse and state media, criticizing the Western liberal order, American dominance, and imposition of cultural and political norms. Since Russia's full-scale invasion of Ukraine, these ideas have become central in Putin's speeches that frame the "collective West" as inherently colonial and imperial. That said, this rhetoric has been employed long before 2022: In December 2004, during

---

[15] Marlene Laruelle, Ivan Grek, and Sergey Davydov, "Culturalizing the Nation: A Quantitative Approach to the Russkii/Rossiiskii Semantic Space in Russia's Political Discourse," *Demokratizatsiya: The Journal of Post-Soviet Democratization* 31, no. 1 (2023): 3–28.

Ukraine's Orange Revolution, Putin said that he didn't want "stern men in pith helmets to give the people who have, figuratively speaking, dark political skin, instructions as to how they should live."[16] One may only notice the mirror game with the West, which also tends to "otherize" Russia by denouncing it as colonial and imperial and portray the country as authoritarian, aggressive, and outdated in its values – a pariah on the global stage lacking self-reflection on its history and positionality.

## About This Element

This Element is not a partisan Element: Written collectively by scholars with different disciplinary backgrounds and visions of Russia, it does not aim at delivering a message of truth on Russia's imperial/colonial identity or deny it. More modestly, it aims at contributing to current debates – many of which are rooted in diverging historical and political claims about the nature of the Russian state – by comprehensively looking at Russia through an imperial lens: It disentangles the elements where that lens makes sense and the ones when it does not, highlights elements shared with European modernity and those diverging, stresses the need for a better exploration of the intersectionality and fluidity of collective and individual identities, the relevance of comparison with other imperial/colonial experiences, and the scholarly tools that social sciences and humanities may offer us to analyze Russia. Above all, it hopes for a heuristically more neutral discussion on the paradigm of "Russia as an empire" that respects the diversity of perspectives expressed by actors themselves. While we hope that this Element offers implications for important debates about Russia's imperial/colonial identity taking place worldwide – whether in Ukraine, Central Asia, or the Global South – our primary empirical focus is on Russia itself.

Therefore, the first three sections focus on providing a brief account of the historical development that Russia underwent since the sixteenth century: first as the Russian Empire (Section 1), then as the core of the Soviet Union (Section 2), and, after 1991, as the Russian Federation (Section 3). This historical overview, spanning several centuries and vast territories, unavoidably maintains a level of generality. However, this concise form serves our intention to illuminate critical tensions inherent in the analysis of Russia as an empire in a conceptually accessible manner, suitable for a diverse readership, ranging from students to policymakers and journalists. These sections do not aim to comprehensively

---

[16] Maria Lipman, "How Russia Has Come to Loathe the West," European Council on Foreign Relations, March 13, 2015, https://ecfr.eu/article/commentary_how_russia_has_come_to_loathe_the_west311346/.

cover the entirety of Russian history. Instead, they accentuate aspects that remain subjects of academic debate but are frequently absent in mainstream discourses.

Section 4 discusses the use of decolonization language as an instrument of foreign politics, which is enrooted in the history of the complex and turbulent relationship between the West and Russia. In the context of intensifying tensions that followed the full-scale invasion of Ukraine, the participants of the decolonization debate, we argue, should be wary of actors who co-opt the discourses of emancipation and justice, not with the intention of deconstructing prevailing power structures, but rather to fortify them or substitute them with new ones.

Section 5 serves as a roadmap to navigate the ongoing scholarly discussions surrounding Russian (neo)colonialism. It spotlights key trajectories, areas of contention, and charts prospective paths for future research. The field has been in development for several decades already, although some authors began receiving credit for their work only recently. The section provides also some ideas for incorporation of critical thought into educational curricula, which could be of use for colleagues involved in teaching.

*Note: This Element has been authored by Adam Lenton and two colleagues who have preferred to remain anonymized given the sensitivity of the topic in Russia.*

## 1 Identity and Empire in Russian History

Disentangling some of the challenges discussed in the introduction requires an examination of Russia's imperial history, which can provide insights into the complex and layered ways in which identities and allegiances evolved in the context of empire. In this section we provide a brief, stylistic overview of Russian imperial expansion from Muscovy in the early sixteenth century through to the Soviet Union, focusing on differing patterns of rule with respect to different territories and different peoples across time.

## Patterns of Empire-Building (1552–1917)

Russian imperial expansion and colonization were uneven, taking place over hundreds of years and across territories inhabited by a diverse range of peoples living under various forms of political organization. While a comprehensive historical account is well beyond the scope of this Element, identifying historical patterns and trends can contextualize questions over the nature of colonization across Russia and the role of ethnic, religious, and other identity cleavages over time, helping to provide insights into how these historical legacies map onto more recent political developments. As we outline, it is difficult to talk about a single imperial experience.

## Early Expansion into the Volga and Siberia

Historians often use 1552 as a point of departure for discussing Russian imperial expansion.[17] At this time the Spanish Empire had recently conquered much of Central and South America and established a small presence in present-day Florida, while Tudor England was engaged in a slow conquest of Ireland, and the Ottoman Empire was approaching its territorial peak, having expanded to much of the Balkans and North Africa. In the case of Russia, 1552 marks the date at which Muscovy[18] became a multiethnic empire, having for the first time conquered and annexed a powerful, culturally distinct rival polity – the Kazan Khanate – a majority-Muslim successor state of the Mongol Golden Horde. While Muscovy had set out upon expansion before the reign of Ivan IV (the Terrible, 1530–84), notably the conquest of the Novgorod Republic in 1478, it was only from 1552 onward that significant numbers of non-Slavic, non-Orthodox peoples became subjects of the tsar.

Muscovy's conquest of Kazan was also significant because it removed the only major geographical barrier separating Muscovy from the steppe and Siberia to the east, while also freeing access to the Volga Delta and the Caspian Sea to the south. As a result, it would take Russian explorers less than a century from the conquest of the Kazan Khanate to reach the Pacific Ocean. Echoing the European conquest of the Americas, Russian expansion eastward into Siberia was driven in large part by private merchants seeking riches, notably furs.[19] While the Russians faced fierce resistance from most of the groups they encountered, Siberia's communities were too small and armed with inferior weaponry to that of the Russians to pose a threat to the advancing forces.[20]

## Expansion to the West

Muscovy also expanded to the west during this period, fighting numerous wars against the Polish-Lithuanian Commonwealth and Sweden, occupying territories whose peoples lived under different political systems and social structures from those encountered to the east of Moscow and in Siberia. Perhaps most

---

[17] See Geoffrey A. Hosking, *Russia: People and Empire, 1552–1917* (Harvard University Press, 1997); Andreas Kappeler, *The Russian Empire: A Multi-Ethnic History* (Taylor & Francis, 2001), 16.

[18] Note that we use the terms "Muscovy" and "Russia" interchangeably to refer to the period of the Tsardom of Russia (1547–1721), while the term "Russian Empire" is used to refer to the imperial period from 1721 onward.

[19] James Forsyth, *A History of the Peoples of Siberia: Russia's North Asian Colony 1581–1990* (Cambridge University Press, 1994), 40.

[20] Kappeler, *The Russian Empire*, 35; W. Bruce Lincoln, *The Conquest of a Continent: Siberia and the Russians* (Cornell University Press, 2007), 42.

significant is the Pereiaslav Agreement in 1654 between Muscovy and the Zaporizhzhian Cossacks, which is widely seen as marking the beginning of Russian involvement in what would become modern-day Ukraine.[21]

Some of the most significant imperial conquests around the Baltic Sea and Gulf of Finland took place under the rule of Peter I (the Great, 1672–1725), under whom the Russian state would radically transform, adopting emergent European social and administrative practices and centralizing the role of the state in war and industry.[22] A widening asymmetry in power between the Russian Empire and its erstwhile rival, Poland–Lithuania, culminated in Poland's eventual dismemberment (by Russia, together with Austria and Prussia) through several stages of partition in 1772, 1793, and 1795, which also saw most of modern-day Ukraine annexed by the Russian Empire, with the important exception of western regions under Austrian rule.[23]

### Russia's Civilizing Mission

In the eighteenth and nineteenth centuries, Russian political elites developed a language of a civilizing mission.[24] This went hand in hand with Enlightenment notions of rationality and order, similar to what the political scientist James Scott terms "high modernism," whereby states seek to reorder both the social and natural worlds.[25] As early as under Peter I, German scholars were hired with the task of "de-barbarizing this vast empire," as Gottfried Wilhelm Leibniz, one of the scholars patronized by Peter I, put it.[26]

This transformation had important consequences for many of the semi-nomadic frontier societies that had enjoyed a degree of autonomy, either as subjects of the tsar or as vassal states of Muscovy. From the Black Sea (the Zaporizhzhian Host) to the Caspian (the Kalmyk Khanate) and the Bashkir and Kazakh steppes to the east, the eighteenth century saw the imposition of direct rule from Russia's new capital of Saint Petersburg, together with the physical

---

[21] Kappeler, *The Russian Empire*, 61.

[22] Hosking, *Russia*, 79–91; Vera Tolz, *Russia: Inventing the Nation* (Arnold, 2001), 29–30; Alfred J. Rieber, *The Struggle for the Eurasian Borderlands* (Cambridge University Press, 2014), 203; Perry Anderson, *Lineages of the Absolutist State* (New Left Books, 1974), 341.

[23] Hosking, *Russia*, 28–29.

[24] Ricarda Vulpius, "The Russian Empire's Civilizing Mission in the Eighteenth Century: A Comparative Perspective," in *Asiatic Russia: Imperial Power in Regional and International Contexts*, ed. Tomohiko Uyama (Routledge, 2012), 18.

[25] James C. Scott, *Seeing Like a State: How Certain Schemes to Improve the Human Condition Have Failed* (Yale University Press, 2020), 4.

[26] Yuri Slezkine, "Naturalists versus Nations: Eighteenth-Century Russian Scholars Confront Ethnic Diversity," in *Russia's Orient: Imperial Borderlands and Peoples 1700–1917*, ed. Daniel R. Brower and Edward J. Lazzerini (Indiana University Press, 1997), 29.

colonization of these territories by sedentary agriculturalists and the eradication of the nomadic way of life.[27]

The shifting approach toward the frontier was partly shaped by Russia's wars with the Ottoman and Persian Empires, but it was also accompanied by a new sense of self and of other as the Russian Empire encountered an internal Orient through its conquests of Muslim-majority Crimea and the North Caucasus. The 1783 conquest of Crimea from the Crimean Khanate was interpreted through a new language of European Enlightenment "civilization," with Russia also using Crimea to craft symbolic claims to be the inheritor of classical Greek antiquity.[28] The conquest of the North Caucasus was slow and brutal, with one prominent historian estimating that almost two million people died from battle or disease for the Russian Empire to annex the region.[29] For Russian military officials, the lack of "civilization" of the peoples they encountered went hand in hand with condonement of extreme political violence.[30] These themes were prominent in the literary works of the time, with famous Russian writers such as Aleksandr Pushkin and Mikhail Lermontov underscoring narratives of European superiority while occasionally sympathizing with "noble" Caucasian "savages."[31]

Russian imperial expansion was quite different in the South Caucasus, where the annexation of Georgia in 1801 and the former Khanate of Yerevan in 1828 was welcomed by many of the local population fearful of domination by the Muslim Persian Empire and the Ottoman Empire.[32] Put differently, while in the North Caucasus Saint Petersburg's "aim was to pacify and incorporate the tribes," in the South Caucasus the aim was "to resolve the problems of the

---

[27] Serhii Plokhy, *The Gates of Europe: A History of Ukraine* (Basic Books, 2017), 140; Michael Khodarkovsky, *Where Two Worlds Met: The Russian State and the Kalmyk Nomads, 1600–1771* (Cornell University Press, 1992); Michael Khodarkovsky, *Russia's Steppe Frontier: The Making of a Colonial Empire, 1500–1800* (Indiana University Press, 2002); Alton S. Donnelly, *The Russian Conquest of Bashkiria 1552–1740* (Yale University Press, 1968); Charles Steinwedel, *Threads of Empire* (Indiana University Press, 2016); Willard Sunderland, *Taming the Wild Field: Colonization and Empire on the Russian Steppe* (Cornell University Press, 2004).

[28] As Andrei Zorin describes, this "Greek project" sought to establish Russia as a direct inheritor of Greek antiquity, rather than via Western intermediaries. See Andrei Zorin, *Kormia dvuglavogo orla ... Literatura i gosudarstvennaia ideologiia v Rossii v posledney treti XVIII–pervoy treti XIX veka* (Novoe literaturnoe obozrenie, 2001).

[29] Michael Khodarkovsky, *Bitter Choices: Loyalty and Betrayal in the Russian Conquest of the North Caucasus* (Cornell University Press, 2011), 12.

[30] Irma Kreiten, "A Colonial Experiment in Cleansing: The Russian Conquest of Western Caucasus, 1856–65," *Journal of Genocide Research* 11, no. 2/3 (June 2009): 217; Walter Richmond, *The Circassian Genocide* (Rutgers University Press, 2013).

[31] Susan Layton, "Nineteenth-Century Russian Mythologies of Caucasian Savagery," in *Russia's Orient: Imperial Borderlands and Peoples, 1700–1917*, ed. Daniel R. Brower and Edward J. Lazzerini (Indiana University Press, 1997), 82; Tolz, *Russia*, 137–38.

[32] Valerie A. Kivelson and Ronald Grigor Suny, *Russia's Empires* (Oxford University Press, 2016), 168–69.

complex frontier by driving out the Ottomans and Iranians, and consolidating Georgian and Armenian states under Russian tutelage."[33]

### Colonization in Central and East Asia

While the Russian Empire had already begun to consolidate direct rule over the steppe lands of modern-day Kazakhstan in the 1730s, the imperial rule over Central Asia expanded steadily throughout the nineteenth century, during roughly the same time period as when Britain established direct rule over much of India (1858), and which ended with the European colonization of much of the African continent in the early 1880s.[34] Russian expansion, however, was not uniform: Some polities were abolished upon conquest (such as the Khanate of Kokand), while others were made protectorates (such as the Khanate of Khiva, or the Emirate of Bukhara) and the Turkmen lands were slowly incorporated in the 1880s.[35] Russian administrators came to see this part of the Empire as more akin to other overseas empires, like the French in Algeria or the British in India, than they did other areas within the Russian Empire.[36]

The Russian Empire also expanded further east, this time at the expense of the Qing Empire. The Treaties of Aigun (1858) and Beijing (1860) ceded much of Manchuria and the Pacific coastline to Saint Petersburg.[37]

## Layered Identities and Loyalties

The previous section described the broad patterns of Russian imperial expansion from the mid sixteenth century to 1917. This section considers the complex identities and loyalties of the people who lived in these diverse regions, as well as their interactions with the imperial center.

### Religion and Conversionary Waves

Prior to the emergence of modern ethnic and nationalist movements, religion was a far more salient and potent element of identity. Eastern Orthodox Christianity was a key pillar of the Muscovite state and the Russian Empire,

---

[33] Rieber, *The Struggle for the Eurasian Borderlands*, 380.

[34] Alexander Morrison, "Introduction: Killing the Cotton Canard and Getting Rid of the Great Game: Rewriting the Russian Conquest of Central Asia, 1814–1895," *Central Asian Survey* 33, no. 2 (April 3, 2014): 131.

[35] Ian W. Campbell, "Russian Rule in Central Asia," in *The Routledge Handbook of Contemporary Central Asia*, ed. Rico Isaacs and Erica Marat (Routledge, 2021), 40–42.

[36] Jeff Sahadeo, *Russian Colonial Society in Tashkent, 1865–1923* (Indiana University Press, 2007), 4–5.

[37] This was accompanied by a short-lived euphoria that the Amur region would be "Russia's Mississippi." See Sören Urbansky, *Beyond the Steppe Frontier* (Princeton University Press, 2020), 30.

in which there was an even stronger fusion between the Orthodox Church and political power than there was between Church and state in the Catholic West.[38] Nevertheless, it is worth acknowledging that the extent to which religious ideology drove Muscovy's expansion remains debated.[39]

The conquest of the Muslim Kazan Khanate in 1552, for instance, was accompanied by mass political violence including the razing of Kazan's mosques and the forced conversion of any Tatars who wished to remain in the city.[40] However, more generally, the Muscovite state lacked the capacity to engage in widespread baptism beyond urban centers and so it widely relied upon co-opting local elites.[41] Thus, throughout much of the 1600s, the situation could be characterized as one of "benign neglect."[42]

The reforms under Peter I, including abolishing the Patriarchate of Moscow and All Rus' and creating the Holy Synod – a congregation of Orthodox church leaders unable to impede the emperor's reforms – further subordinated religious institutions to the control of the state, which began to discriminate along religious lines and employ coercive measures to convert during the eighteenth century.[43] Conversion to Orthodoxy, however, was usually only nominal, chosen by individuals due to specific economic and social incentives, with previous animist and traditional practices remaining prevalent until the nineteenth century. Only then did syncretism arouse the concern of state officials and more comprehensive policies were adopted to instill Orthodoxy in non-Russian populations.[44]

Missionary activity was most active (and successful) among groups practicing polytheistic and animist religions and least successful among areas where Islam and Catholicism were most entrenched. This was in part due to the conscious decision to avoid intensifying tensions – missionary activities in the North Caucasus, for instance, were occasionally permitted in areas where Islam coexisted with polytheistic practices, such as among the

---

[38] Burbank and Cooper, *Empires in World History*, 193.

[39] See Edward Louis Keenan, "Muscovy and Kazan: Some Introductory Remarks on the Patterns of Steppe Diplomacy," *Slavic Review* 26, no. 4 (1967): 548–58; "Muscovite Political Folkways," *The Russian Review* 45, no. 2 (1986): 115–81; Donald Ostrowski, *Muscovy and the Mongols: Cross-Cultural Influences on the Steppe Frontier, 1304–1589* (Cambridge University Press, 2002).

[40] See Azade-Ayşe Rorlich, *The Volga Tatars: A Profile in National Resilience* (Hoover Institution Press, 1986), 39, 207.

[41] Matthew P. Romaniello, *The Elusive Empire: Kazan and the Creation of Russia, 1552–1671* (University of Wisconsin Press, 2012), 37–39; Kappeler, *The Russian Empire*, 28.

[42] Michael Khodarkovsky, "The Conversion of Non-Christians in Early Modern Russia," in *Of Religion and Empire: Missions, Conversion, and Tolerance in Tsarist Russia*, ed. Robert Geraci and Michael Khodarkovsky (Cornell University Press, 2018), 116.

[43] Tolz, *Russia*, 37; Kappeler, *The Russian Empire*, 31; Khodarkovsky, "The Conversion," 116.

[44] Khodarkovsky, "The Conversion," 117; Kappeler, *The Russian Empire*, 31.

Ossetians, but not in other areas such as Dagestan or Chechnya, which were predominantly Muslim.[45]

Russian Orthodox Christianity was not the only proselytizing religion in the Empire. It faced competition in southeastern Siberia from Tibetan and Mongolian Buddhist lamas, who were successful in converting large numbers of Buryats, as well as the Tuvans (who were at this time part of the Qing Empire) to Tibetan Buddhism.[46] The Volga region, too, saw renewed Muslim conversion in the wake of Catherine II's toleration reforms, with particular success among the then-nominally Orthodox Chuvash people.[47] In the North Caucasus, Islam strengthened as a result of the Russian military conquest and turned into a rallying force for resistance, in particular among Sufi orders such as the Naqshbandi and Qadiri, which became prominent in the nineteenth century.[48]

An important respite in missionary activity took place under Catherine II. In 1767, Muslims and animists were invited to participate in her Legislative Commission, while mosques were rebuilt and Volga Tatars enjoyed something of a renaissance, in part because she "believed that Tatars could play a civilizing role among the animist peoples of the Russian Empire."[49] The Orenburg Muslim Spiritual Assembly in 1788 and the Muslim Ecclesiastical Council in 1789 were created as a means of furthering state control over the Empire's Muslim subjects while permitting religious freedom.[50] The state thus acquired a workable bureaucracy for its Muslim subjects, which, in turn, transformed religious leaders into intermediaries and agents of empire.[51]

To the west, hostility between Poland and Russia mapped onto a religious struggle between Catholic and Orthodox Christianity.[52] Relations with Catholicism were volatile. While the aftermath of the French Revolution led to a temporary thaw (amid the perceived greater threat from revolutionary republicanism), from the Partitions of Poland and "until the demise of Imperial Russia in

---

[45] Firouzeh Mostashari, "Colonial Dilemmas: Russian Policies in the Muslim Caucasus," in *Of Religion and Empire: Missions, Conversion, and Tolerance in Tsarist Russia*, ed. Robert P. Geraci and Michael Khodarkovsky (Cornell University Press, 2001), 229–49.

[46] Kappeler, *The Russian Empire*, 149.

[47] Agnès Nilüfer Kefeli, *Becoming Muslim in Imperial Russia: Conversion, Apostasy, and Literacy* (Cornell University Press, 2014), 22.

[48] Uwe Halbach, "Islam in the North Caucasus," *Archives de Sciences Sociales Des Religions*, no. 115 (2001): 93–110.

[49] Kappeler, *The Russian Empire*, 169; Rorlich, *The Volga Tatars*, 42.

[50] Galina Yemelianova, "Russia's Umma and Its Muftis," *Religion, State and Society* 31, no. 2 (June 2003): 139–50.

[51] Mustafa Tuna, *Imperial Russia's Muslims: Islam, Empire, and European Modernity, 1788–1914* (Cambridge University Press, 2015), 45.

[52] Theodore R. Weeks, "Between Rome and Tsargrad: The Uniate Church in Imperial Russia," in *Of Religion and Empire*, ed. Robert P. Geraci and Michael Khodarkovsky (Cornell University Press, 2001), 73–74.

1917, the Catholic and Polish questions plagued and complicated Russian administration."[53] The Russian Empire also sought to convert members of the Ruthenian Uniate Church, sandwiched between Catholicism and Orthodoxy and prominent in the territories of modern-day Lithuania, Belarus, and western Ukrainian territories between Poland and Romania.[54]

The nineteenth century saw increased attempts to convert and assimilate non-Russians to Orthodoxy, and a more standardized approach to Russification as "it became increasingly difficult to be both a loyal subject of the Russian tsar and a non-Orthodox believer."[55] This was reflected in the ideological doctrine formulated by imperial Minister of Education Sergey Uvarov in 1833 – "Orthodoxy, autocracy, and nationality" – which served as the tsarist regime's response to the French republican slogan of *liberté, égalité, fraternité*.[56] Missionary activity intensified, while in the Volga region, new educational establishments aimed to teach in local languages such as Tatar and Chuvash as a means of assimilation into Orthodoxy. This approach would later be echoed by the Soviet Union's attempts to foster Soviet identity through national education – which would be "national in form, socialist in content."[57]

Yet greater assimilationist measures also coexisted with a degree of accommodation toward some subjects. While it is difficult to speak of a single "Muslim policy" during this time,[58] the Russian Empire blended civic law, customary law (*adat'*), and sharia law in its Muslim regions.[59] By the early twentieth century, the Russian Empire had more Muslim subjects than did the Ottoman Empire, plus several million Catholics, Jews, and Lutherans, though this diversity was not accompanied by uniform toleration.[60]

## Migration and Settlement

The Empire's expansion was accompanied by significant migration and settlement. Migration was limited in the early modern period during Muscovy's expansion to the Volga region and Siberia, with the partial exception of

---

[53] Ibid., 72.　　[54] Ibid., 72.　　[55] Ibid., 74.

[56] Laura Engelstein, *Slavophile Empire: Imperial Russia's Illiberal Path* (Cornell University Press, 2011), 5.

[57] Kappeler, *The Russian Empire*, 262; Terry Dean Martin, *The Affirmative Action Empire: Nations and Nationalism in the Soviet Union, 1923–1939* (Cornell University Press, 2001).

[58] Paolo Sartori and Danielle Ross, eds, *Shari'a in the Russian Empire: The Reach and Limits of Islamic Law in Central Eurasia, 1550–1917* (Edinburgh University Press, 2020).

[59] Robert D. Crews, *For Prophet and Tsar: Islam and Empire in Russia and Central Asia* (Harvard University Press, 2006); Michael Kemper, "'Adat Against Shari'a: Russian Approaches toward Daghestani 'Customary Law' in the 19th Century," *Ab Imperio*, no. 3 (2005): 147–73; Egor Lazarev, "Laws in Conflict: Legacies of War, Gender, and Legal Pluralism in Chechnya," *World Politics* 71, no. 4 (October 2019): 667–709.

[60] Crews, *For Prophet and Tsar*, 4.

Kazan, the former capital of the Kazan Khanate, which was razed to the ground in 1552 and whose surrounding lands were settled by members of the Muscovite elite.[61] Sizeable peasant populations already existing in much of the middle Volga region meant that there was relatively little settlement by Russians during this period.[62]

Aside from small trading settlements and forts, migration further east to Siberia was relatively minor before the nineteenth century, consisting of forced labor or banishment as well as small groups of peasants fleeing serfdom for the relative freedom that Siberia – far from the reach of the state – could offer.[63] Like in the Americas, this also included individuals fleeing religious persecution, such as the Old Believers,[64] many of whom settled in what would become modern-day Altai and Tuva, in the middle of the southernmost part of Siberia.[65] While in 1800 there were fewer than 600,000 Russians in Siberia, between 1897 and 1911 alone over 3.5 million people moved there from European Russia.[66]

When it came to the steppe frontiers to the south and east, whose nomadic and semi-nomadic societies had submitted to Russian suzerainty, migration was initially discouraged by the tsarist authorities, and diplomatic correspondence would often raise issues related to the migration or mixing of populations.[67] In a later reversal of policy, migrants were encouraged to settle as the government sought to bring these areas under direct rule during the eighteenth century, dramatically altering the steppe and its societies. This went hand in hand with Enlightenment-era thinking that saw such settlement as part of a civilizing mission, illustrated by Prince Grigory Potemkin's 1786 letter to Catherine II regarding Novorossiya (today's eastern and southern Ukraine): "This country, with your care, has been turned from a place of uninhabited steppes into a garden of abundance, from a lair of beasts to a pleasing refuge for peoples from all countries."[68]

---

[61] Vil'iam V. Pokhlebkin, *Tatary i Rus': 360 let otnoshenii Rusi s tatarskimi gosudarstvami v XIII–XVI vv. 1238–1598 gg: Ot bitvy na r. Sit' do pokoreniia Sibiri: spravochnik* (Mezhdunarodnye otnosheniia, 2000), 139.

[62] Andreas Kappeler, *Die Tschuwaschen: Ein Volk im Schatten der Geschichte* (Böhlau Verlag Köln Weimar, 2016), 65; Matthew P. Romaniello, "Grant, Settle, Negotiate: Military Servitors in the Middle Volga Region," in *Peopling the Russian Periphery: Borderland Colonization in Eurasian History*, ed. Nicholas B. Breyfogle, Abby Schrader, and Willard Sunderland (Routledge, 2007).

[63] Lincoln, *Conquest of a Continent*, 164–65, 256–57.

[64] Old Believers were a group of Orthodox Russian dissenters who refused to accept the liturgical reforms undertaken in the 1650s.

[65] Dmitrii A. Funk and Nikolai A. Alekseev, eds, *Tiurkskie narody Vostochnoy Sibiri* (Nauka, 2008), 25.

[66] Lincoln, *Conquest of a Continent*, 257–58.

[67] Forsyth, *A History of the Peoples of Siberia*, 117; Khodarkovsky, *Where Two Worlds Met*, 105–06.

[68] Quoted in Sunderland, *Taming the Wild Field*, 113.

At the invitation of Catherine II, large numbers of German colonists settled in the steppe lands in the lower Volga and Novorossiya, which by 1815 counted 1.5 million inhabitants: a multiethnic mixture of Ukrainian peasants as well as significant numbers of Russian, German, Jewish, and Greek colonists.[69] The Black Sea coastline in the North Caucasus, too, was settled by Slavic migrants in the wake of the conquest of the Caucasus and the expulsion of the Indigenous population.[70] In Bashkiria, a region at the southern end of the Ural Mountains, previous bans on the selling of land to non-Bashkirs were revoked in the nineteenth century, leading to the mass influx of Slavic migrants, who comprised over a quarter of the population by the 1740s.[71] The nomadic Kalmyks' pastoral lands were increasingly restricted as Russian fortifications developed and agriculturalists settled in the Volga Delta, leading to the former's mass exodus in 1771.[72]

To summarize, migration and colonization looked very different in various parts of the Russian Empire. In some cases, it is possible to discern colonizers more clearly from the colonized, whereas in others they may have overlapped.

### Imperial Intermediaries

Indeed, Russian imperial expansion would not have been possible without the involvement of influential intermediaries in the regions. The co-optation of local political elites (often going hand in hand with conversion to Orthodoxy) was one of many tools – together with the signing of protectorate treaties that allowed for gradual annexation, and military force – which Muscovy used in order to expand.[73] Marriage alliances integrated elites into personalized patronal "pyramids," while land grants further consolidated these personalized systems of exchange.[74] Meanwhile, elite and diplomatic interactions between Russia and the frontier societies would often be interpreted according to both sides' traditions of political thinking, which could – and often did – lead to misunderstandings.[75]

The gap between Russian elite and popular culture was itself significant and became even more so under Peter I and afterward, as the aristocracy "drew its inspiration and substance from contemporary Western civilization."[76] Thus

---

[69] Kappeler, *The Russian Empire*, 51, 123.

[70] Timur Natkhov, "Colonization and Development: The Long-Term Effect of Russian Settlement in the North Caucasus, 1890s–2000s," *Journal of Comparative Economics* 43, no. 1 (February 2015): 80.

[71] Sunderland, *Taming the Wild Field*, 67.

[72] Khodarkovsky, *Where Two Worlds Met*, 140, 232.   [73] Kappeler, *The Russian Empire*, 18.

[74] Burbank and Cooper, *Empires in World History*, 193; Henry E. Hale, *Patronal Politics: Eurasian Regime Dynamics in Comparative Perspective* (Cambridge University Press, 2014), 43.

[75] Khodarkovsky, *Where Two Worlds Met*, 73.

[76] Marc Raeff, *Understanding Imperial Russia*, reprint ed. (Columbia University Press, 1984), 23.

certain groups of nobles – in particular, Baltic Germans – were disproportionately prominent in high-level posts for much of the eighteenth and nineteenth centuries and standard-bearers for a state patriotism that was much farther removed from mass culture than is modern-day nationalism.[77]

Beyond the aristocracy, traders and educators were important intermediaries and agents of empire. Volga Tatar merchants and Islamic authorities occupied a prominent role as middlemen in the Urals and Central Asia.[78] Russian rule also granted Armenian merchants tax exemptions and travel privileges, making them valuable intermediaries in the wider Caucasus region and fostering an emerging national intelligentsia.[79]

## Estate, Ethnicity, Nation, and Class

As discussed earlier, religion and estate-based differences were prominent identity markers throughout much of the Russian Empire's history. It is only in the nineteenth century that ethnicity and nation emerged as even more powerful identities that could mobilize large numbers of people.

The idea of national self-determination as the heart of nationalism was a relatively recent phenomenon.[80] This was seen as particularly threatening to Saint Petersburg, given the cultural gaps not only among the Empire's various subject populations but also that between its ruling elites and the Russian masses. This anxiety was heightened by new political challenges to imperial rule, especially in Poland, which had undergone national mobilization during the Napoleonic era with sizeable revolts against Russian rule.[81]

Moreover, since Polish nationalism made claims on East Slavic territories that Saint Petersburg saw as politically Russian, this spurred tsarist elites to devote considerable efforts to fostering popular support for the regime.[82] Imperial elites were not alone in this endeavor: The early nineteenth century saw writers, historians, and aristocrats contemplate new forms of political

---

[77] Nicholas I's secret police was commonly known as the "German department" in the mid nineteenth century. See Hosking, *Russia*, 160.

[78] Danielle Ross, *Tatar Empire: Kazan's Muslims and the Making of Imperial Russia* (Indiana University Press, 2020).

[79] Kivelson and Suny, *Russia's Empires*, 169; Ronald Grigor Suny, *Looking toward Ararat: Armenia in Modern History* (Indiana University Press, 1993), 57–58, 69.

[80] See Harris Mylonas and Maya Tudor, *Varieties of Nationalism: Communities, Narratives, Identities* (Cambridge University Press, 2023).

[81] Serhii Plokhy, *Lost Kingdom: The Quest for Empire and the Making of the Russian Nation* (Basic Books, 2017), 80.

[82] Aleksei Miller, *The Ukrainian Question: The Russian Empire and Nationalism in the Nineteenth Century* (Central European University Press, 2003), 25.

participation, sovereignty, and solidarity with intellectual zest and occasionally revolutionary fervor, too – exemplified by the Decembrist Revolt of 1825.[83]

While ethnic and national identities gained prominence during this time, they were not pertinent all the time or even in most situations. Most people identified themselves as being from a particular place, or would identify themselves according to their faith. Moreover, subjects in the Empire were highly stratified according to social estate, including within the imperial bureaucracy.[84]

One important characteristic that would endure into the Soviet understanding of ethnicity was language: Language was used by the Empire to classify its subjects, most visibly in the 1897 census, which recorded respondents' faith and native language.

By the dawn of the twentieth century, nascent national movements were emerging across the Empire, pushing for cultural and spiritual revival. Some became politically represented in the newly formed Duma following the 1905 Revolution, which broke out as a consequence of Russia's defeat in the Russo-Japanese War, and led to demands for reform along the lines of a constitutional monarchy.[85] National movements were most successful, however, when cultural demands overlapped with other grievances such as economic status or land ownership.[86] Regional movements have not always been exclusively ethnic, either: one can point to the emergence of prominent Siberian regionalism in the nineteenth century, a phenomenon that will reemerge in early post-Soviet Russia.[87] Yet it was this rising tide of national self-consciousness that Lenin and the Bolsheviks consciously sought to co-opt in the wake of October Revolution in 1917.

## Conclusion

This section has presented a brief overview of Russian imperial history and the identities of its peoples. Specifically, we suggest two important takeaways.

---

[83] The Decembrists, made up of nobles and officers, led an unsuccessful uprising after the death of Tsar Alexander I. See Ilya Gerasimov, Marina Mogil'ner, and Sergey Glebov, *Novaia imperskaia istoriia Severnoi Evrazii* (Ab Imperio, 2017), 185–86.

[84] Estate-based identities also had an enduring effect well into the Soviet period. See Tomila V. Lankina, *The Estate Origins of Democracy in Russia* (Cambridge University Press, 2021).

[85] Kappeler, *The Russian Empire*, 328–69.

[86] For example, the centrality of land ownership to the Bashkir movement, or of socioeconomic status in Georgia, or the alliance of Ukrainian peasants and the Central Rada in the Ukrainian People's Republic; see Steinwedel, *Threads of Empire*, 219; Ronald Grigor Suny, *The Making of the Georgian Nation, Second Edition* (Indiana University Press, 1994), 145; Plokhy, *The Gates of Europe*, 206.

[87] Susan Smith-Peter, *Imagining Russian Regions: Subnational Identity and Civil Society in Nineteenth-Century Russia* (Brill, 2017); Yoshiko Herrera, *Imagined Economies: The Sources of Russian Regionalism* (Cambridge University Press, 2005).

First, experiences of empire and colonization differed greatly across space and time. This becomes apparent when examining the different approaches taken toward expansion, as well as the policies enacted with respect to the societies and peoples who became part of the Russian Empire – including the complex role of ethnic Russians, as summarized in Box 1. While in some cases colonization implied the physical settlement of non-native populations, in other cases there was little settler colonization at all; while in the North Caucasus imperial expansion was accompanied by political violence, including mass deportations, the situation was different in the South Caucasus. Discussions of decolonization in the Russian context, therefore, ought to be aware of these historical and regional differences to better understand ways in which it makes sense (or not) to talk of decolonization in the singular and with reference to the Russian Federation as a whole.

Second, identities and allegiances were (and, as the next section will show, still are) complex and intersectional, cross-cutting religious, ethnic, and class divides. Great caution should be taken, therefore, when generalizing based upon group identity, or if a given identity category is essentialized as unchanging, predominant, or understood to be more important than others throughout history. Viewing decolonization from an ethnocentric lens risks oversimplification and obscures important ways in which people negotiate and transform their identities and relation to the state.

---

Box 1: The "Russian Question": Ethnic Russians in the Empire(s)

Any discussion of empire and history requires addressing the so-called "Russian question."[88] Central to this is whether it is possible to define the Russian Empire, the Soviet Union, and even the Russian Federation as Russian imperial polities in an ethnic or nationalist sense. While it is not possible to fully address the vast literature on Russian nationalism and empire – nor is this our aim – some context is important for understanding some of the tensions presented in this Element.

On the one hand, ethnic Russians have always been the core of the tsarist polities. The unity of dynasty, Church, and people meant that there was a tangible sense of Russianness even before the emergence of modern-day nationalism that went hand in hand with identification with the tsar and the

---

[88] Some influential works on Russian nationalism in the context of empire include but are not limited to Tolz, *Russia*; Alexei Miller, "The Romanov Empire and the Russian Nation," in *Nationalizing Empires*, ed. Alexei Miller and Stefan Berger (Central European University Press, 2015), 309–68; Roman Szporluk, "Dilemmas of Russian Nationalism," *Problems of Communism* 38, no. 4 (1989): 15–35; Marlene Laruelle, *Russian Nationalism: Imaginaries, Doctrines, and Political Battlefields* (Routledge, 2018).

regime.[89] In terms of numbers, ethnic Russians were a clear plurality of subjects of the tsar, though this figure shifted considerably over time. Notions of Russian superiority also pervaded the Empire's expansion; assimilation to Russian Orthodoxy and acquisition of Russian cultural traits, including language, were pursued both by local elites as well as the central government with relation to other ethnic and religious groups.[90]

On the other hand, however, the Russian Empire – indeed, like most multiethnic empires – pursued a variegated approach to managing diversity, and was hostile to any manifestations of nationalism that might undermine tsarist rule.[91] The aristocracy was increasingly removed from the masses in the early modern period, including linguistically, best illustrated by the use of French in the eighteenth and nineteenth centuries.[92] At the mass level, serfdom bound millions of Russians to conditions of hereditary servitude, and to their estate owners for much of the imperial period prior to its abolition in 1861 by Tsar Alexander II.[93] These serfs were generally underprivileged when compared with non-Russian peasants, who in the Volga and Ural regions were "state serfs" considered personally free albeit tied to the land. Consequently, many peasants would seek to escape serfdom by fleeing to the imperial frontier and joining local Cossack units, predominantly in Siberia in the seventeenth century, Ukraine in the early eighteenth century, and then the Caucasus Mountains and Kazakh steppes in the late eighteenth and early nineteenth centuries.[94]

The position of the Soviet Union toward ethnic Russians was also characterized by tension. The Bolsheviks declared war on "great Russian chauvinism"[95] and systematically promoted the national consciousness of

---

[89] Dominic Lieven, *Empire: The Russian Empire and Its Rivals* (Yale University Press, 2002), 253–55.

[90] Kappeler, *The Russian Empire*, 262.

[91] As one historian put it, "in Russia state-building obstructed nation-building." See Hosking, *Russia*, xxiv.

[92] Derek Offord, Vladislav Rjéoutski, and Gesine Argent, *The French Language in Russia: A Social, Political, Cultural, and Literary History* (Amsterdam University Press, 2018).

[93] Hans-Heinrich Nolte and Elena Smolarz, "Slavery and Serfdom in Muscovy and the Russian Empire," in *The Palgrave Handbook of Global Slavery throughout History*, ed. Damian A. Pargas and Juliane Schiel (Springer, 2023), 287.

[94] Ibid., 290.

[95] See the following translation: "Lenin: 'I Declare War to Death on Great Russian Chauvinism," *The Militant* 82, no. 48 (2018), https://themilitant.com/2018/12/19/lenin-i-declare-war-to-death-on-great-russian-chauvinism/.

ethnic minorities, assigning specific administrative territories to certain ethnic groups. On the other hand, Russians were also elevated to the position of "first among equals," while non-Russian Soviet citizens were expected to acquire Russian attributes such as language. Starting from the 1970s, decolonization discourses gained traction among dissident ethnic Russian circles, as well as post-Soviet popular discourse and foreign academic debate,[96] in which Russians are presented as the nation the most repressed by the Soviet regime. Such tensions remain prominent in the Russian Federation, where the community is described as a "multinational people"; ethnic Russians are in some aspects elevated to a privileged position, while Russian nationalists maintain that ethnic Russians are underprivileged.

## 2 The Soviet Rule: Decolonial in Form, Colonial in Content?

Was the Soviet Union a (colonial) empire? This question extends beyond academic discussions to popular media and policy debates. The prevailing consensus leans toward categorizing it as such, albeit with certain distinctive characteristics. Three key aspects are commonly highlighted as distinguishing the Soviet Union from other colonial empires, which either did not prioritize radical transformation and modernization or focused primarily on establishing capitalist systems of colonial dominance: (1) Soviet policymakers did not construct a single ethnicity-centered nation, instead supporting and elevating certain non-Russian ethnic groups; (2) the core of the Soviet experiment was a large-scale endeavor at modernization, involving a radical transformation of existing economic structures, social norms, and cultural practices for both the "core" national group and "peripheral" ones, to create an alternative to the dominant model of capitalist economic relations; (3) on a global scale, the Soviet Union portrayed itself (and sometimes also acted) as an anti-imperialist and anticolonial communist power.[97]

Nevertheless, these three aspects belie the extent to which the Soviet experiment was at the same time imperial, whether through the rigid imposition of a hierarchy of primordial ethnic identities, the mass violence and repressions

---

[96] Geofrey Hosking, *Rulers and Victims: The Russians in the Soviet Union* (Harvard University Press, 2009), 136.

[97] Karen Barkey and Mark von Hagen, eds, *After Empire: Multiethnic Societies and Nation-Building: The Soviet Union and the Russian, Ottoman, and Habsburg Empires* (Westview Press, 1997); Martin, *The Affirmative Action Empire*; Dominic Lieven, "The Russian Empire and the Soviet Union as Imperial Polities," *Journal of Contemporary History* 30, no. 4 (1995): 607–36; Mark R. Beissinger, *Nationalist Mobilization and the Collapse of the Soviet State* (Cambridge University Press, 2002).

that accompanied the Soviet modernization drive, or the tension between Soviet anti-imperial rhetoric and its political dominance over Communist parties and states, particularly in Central and Eastern Europe. How can we make sense of this complex legacy?

## Population

### *1920s–1930s*

The 1917 Russian Revolution can be perceived as an initial liberation movement aimed at dismantling the imperial institutions established by the tsars – a movement that indeed did have some decolonial features.[98] However, unlike other European empires, such as the Habsburg or Ottoman, which disintegrated following World War I, the collapse of the Russian Empire did not result in the formation of separate nation-states for more than a few months. Instead, a nominally federal state, the Soviet Union, emerged in December 1922 from the former imperial structure following the Bolshevik victory in the Russian Civil War. It sought to drastically change the social organization of its population, guided by the vision of overcoming ethnic nationalism and advancing toward a classless communist future.

To confront the rising tide of non-Russian nationalist movements that they had inherited from the imperial state, the Bolsheviks systematically promoted the national consciousness of ethnic minorities and assigned specific administrative territories to given ethnic groups. These top–down programs strengthened the connection between ethnicity and a particular territory and granted the "titular" ethnic groups greater rights and autonomy – including *within* union republics – which Terry Martin describes as an "affirmative action" empire.[99] In "form," the state endorsed ethnic nationalism through numerous actions: the creation of national literature canons, language standardization, folklore promotion, and the appointment of national cadres to leadership positions in respective republics (under the slogan of "indigenization" known as *korenizatsiia*). However, these programs' "content," claims of sovereignty, independence, national superiority, cultural – especially religious – distinctiveness, or ethnic nationalism was actively suppressed.

Even though the Soviet Union engaged in de facto nation-building,[100] the Bolsheviks believed that national identity was a purely temporary stage along

---

[98] Joshua A. Sanborn, *Imperial Apocalypse: The Great War and the Destruction of the Russian Empire* (Oxford University Press, 2014).

[99] Martin, *The Affirmative Action Empire*.

[100] Dmitry Gorenburg, *Minority Ethnic Mobilization in the Russian Federation* (Cambridge University Press, 2003), 30, 37.

the path of historical development leading to a communist society.[101] By granting the "forms" of nationhood, it would be possible to both disarm anti-Bolshevik nationalism *and* inculcate socialist thinking across the Soviet Union, thus accelerating the transition to communism.[102]

Soviet nationalities policy contributed to the collectivizing of individual rights: Individuals were endowed with rights only because they belonged to a certain group. For example, Stalin defined the nation as "a historically constituted, stable community of people, formed on the basis of a common language, territory, economic life, and psychological makeup manifested in a common culture"[103] such as that territory thus became the guarantee of the Indigenousness of the people, while language and "psychological makeup" enabled an essentialist and naturalist reading of the community. The hierarchization of national groups, the obligatory and exclusive allotment of a singular identity, and the obsession with classification would drive the nationalities policy of the Soviet regime until its disappearance.[104]

Whereas in the 1920s, Soviet rationales privileged a diversity of identifications, particularly among small groups, a policy change occurred by the mid 1930s once Stalin established full power over the Communist Party and Soviet state structures. The Soviet leadership reduced the number of officially recognized nationalities, reversed Russification policies, and abandoned indigenization. During this period, Stalin initiated extensive population displacements and reorganizations, leading to a level of political violence that was unprecedented in scale. During the collectivization campaign (most intensive between 1929 and 1933), regardless of their nationality, income, or amount of property, many Soviet farmers – labeled *kulaks* – were relocated to Siberia and Central Asia, and many were sent to labor colonies and camps. The excesses of industrialization led to large-scale shortages, including provisions, which – coupled with crop shortages – contributed to the Soviet famine of 1931–34, marked by widespread starvation in grain-producing regions like Ukraine and Kazakhstan.[105]

Individual ethnic groups once seen as supporters of communism became targets for deportation and ethnic cleansing as the categorization of so-called enemies of the people shifted from Marxist-Leninist, class-based terms to

---

[101] Francine Hirsch, *Empire of Nations: Ethnographic Knowledge and the Making of the Soviet Union* (Cornell University Press, 2005).

[102] Martin, *The Affirmative Action Empire*.

[103] Joseph Stalin, "Marxism and the National Question," in *The Essential Stalin: Major Theoretical Writings 1905–1952*, ed. Bruce Franklin (Croom Helm, 1973), 60.

[104] Yuri Slezkine, "The USSR as a Communal Apartment, or How a Socialist State Promoted Ethnic Particularism," *Slavic Review* 53, no. 2 (Summer 1994): 444.

[105] Some scholars define these famines as genocides that targeted specific ethnic populations, while others emphasize class dynamics. Most prominent is the case of the famine in Ukraine (*Holodomor*), defined by the Ukrainian parliament as an act of genocide in 2006.

ethnic-based ones.[106] The deportations first affected ethnic groups in the sensitive border regions: Ingrian Finns (1929–31 and 1935–39), Finnish people in Karelia (1940–41, 1944), Poles (1939–41 and 1944–45), Kola Norwegians (1940–42), and Far East Koreans (1937). After the Nazi invasion of June 1941, the mass violence scaled up to target Volga Germans, Crimean Tatars, Crimean Greeks, Kalmyks, Balkars, Karachays, Meskhetian Turks, Karakalpaks, Chechens, and Ingush, all suspected of collaborating with the enemy.[107] Deportations also occurred in Soviet-occupied Estonia, Latvia, and Lithuania between 1940 and 1953.[108] These deportations significantly changed both the demographic makeup of the territories these groups were from, as well as those territories where they were sent. Some of the most significant changes took place in territories such as Kazakhstan and the Baltic states, where many of the deported nationalities from across the Soviet Union were sent and where many Russian settlers moved, respectively.[109]

Between 1941 and 1953, close to two million Soviet citizens were deported to Central Asia and Siberia. These deportations, based on political and ethnic criteria, responded to several objectives: punish populations considered "traitors," close domestic ranks in the name of the fight against "fifth columns," and accelerate the colonization of Central Asian and Siberian lands. Hence, Volga Germans and certain displaced persons were massively used in strategic industrial complexes in the region. Other peoples, such as Koreans, were employed in the agricultural *kolkhozes*, particularly the cotton and sugar-producing ones, as well as rice plantations, which required vast amounts of labor. In 1945, more than half a million Japanese war prisoners were also sent to the Gulag labor camps and then forced to work on major Soviet building sites.[110]

Next to ethnicity-specific violence, the state conducted extensive political repression. The Red Terror during the Civil War led to an estimated two million deaths, with about 100,000–200,000 individuals executed.[111] Under Stalin, the Great Purge (1937–38) targeted not only Communist Party members but also peasants, ethnic

---

[106] Martin, *The Affirmative Action Empire*.

[107] Robert Conquest, *The Harvest of Sorrow: Soviet Collectivization and the Terror-Famine* (Oxford University Press, 1986).

[108] Violeta Davoliūtė and Tomas Balkelis, eds, *Narratives of Exile and Identity: Soviet Deportation Memoirs from the Baltic States* (Central European University Press, 2018).

[109] Ali İğmen, "Soviet Central Asia," in *Central Asia: Contexts for Understanding*, ed. David W. Montgomery (University of Pittsburgh Press, 2022), 126.

[110] Viktor Kirillov and Natal'ia Matveeva, "Trudmobilizovannye nemtsy na Urale: sostoianie i novye aspekty issledovaniia problem," in *Nachal'nyi period Velikoi Otechestvennoi voiny i deportatsiia rossiiskikh nemtsev*, ed. Arkadii German (MSNK-Press, 2011), 627–55; Michael Gelb, "An Early Soviet Ethnic Deportation: The Far-Eastern Koreans," *The Russian Review* 54, no. 3 (July 1995): 389–412.

[111] Evan Mawdsley, *The Russian Civil War* (Birlinn, 2011), 341–47.

minority leaders, and unaffiliated individuals – the death toll estimates from the Great Purge range from around 900,000 to nearly 1.2 million.[112] Pervasive police surveillance, paranoia, and incarceration characterized this period. The Gulag system imprisoned approximately fourteen million people from 1930 to 1953, with an estimated 1.5 to 1.7 million dying during incarceration or shortly after release.[113]

The repressive machine inflicted a powerful blow against religious networks. Particularly, the Orthodox Church[114] and Islamic leadership[115] were heavily affected by terror and oppression campaigns before World War II. Muslim institutions and traditions, which form the foundation of the entire pre-Soviet culture and thought of the non-Orthodox population in the Volga Urals, Caucasus, and Central Asia, were drastically altered.[116] State-sponsored atheism was also promoted with regard to other major religions, though as part of the Soviet Union's nationalities policy, religion was in some cases tolerated in a folkloristic way.[117]

Practically every citizen of the Soviet Union was subjected to top–down, drastic, and rapid social engineering measures. The Soviet forced modernization project was an act of violence that gave rise to severe historical traumas. Specifically, it restructured the ethnic groups of the Empire, recreated some peoples anew, and generally included all peoples of the USSR in its universalist historical project. Disruptive language reforms, the creation and rewriting of local histories, standardization of local cultures, and a dramatic loss in transgenerational and family memory were often conducted without the inclusion of community members at large, resulting in the loss of traditional community ties and lifestyles, and the extinction of smaller communities that did not fit into the state nationalities policy.[118]

---

[112] David R. Shearer, *Stalin and War, 1918–1953: Patterns of Repression, Mobilization, and External Threat* (Taylor & Francis, 2023), 33.

[113] Golfo Illness Alexopoulos, *Inhumanity in Stalin's Gulag* (Yale University Press, 2017), 153.

[114] Daniela Kalkandjieva, *The Russian Orthodox Church, 1917–1948: From Decline to Resurrection* (Routledge, 2014).

[115] Michael Kemper, "The Soviet Discourse on the Origin and Class Character of Islam, 1923–1933," *Die Welt des Islams* 49, no. 1 (2009): 1–48.

[116] Shoshana Keller, *To Moscow, Not Mecca: The Soviet Campaign Against Islam in Central Asia, 1917–1941* (Greenwood Publishing Group, 2001); Eren Tasar, *Soviet and Muslim: The Institutionalization of Islam in Central Asia* (Oxford University Press, 2017); Stéphane A. Dudoignon and Christian Noack, *Allah's Kolkhozes: Migration, De-Stalinisation, Privatisation and the New Muslim Congregations in the Soviet Realm (1950s–2000s)* (Schwarz, 2014).

[117] Burbank and Cooper, *Empires in World History*, 397.

[118] E.g., Michael G. Smith, *Language and Power in the Creation of the USSR, 1917–1953* (Walter de Gruyter, 1998); Alfrid K. Bustanov, *Soviet Orientalism and the Creation of Central Asian Nations* (Routledge, 2014); Botakoz Kassymbekova, *Despite Cultures: Early Soviet Rule in Tajikistan* (University of Pittsburgh Press, 2016); Audrey Altstadt, *The Politics of Culture in Soviet Azerbaijan, 1920–40* (Routledge, 2016).

In its early years, the Soviet system was seen as progressive with regard to gender ideologies: Equal gender rights were mandatory under the law, the state supported and legitimized women's presence in the public sphere through education, work, and political representation, the divorce process was simplified, and abortion was legalized. However, in practice, the development of women's political rights and participation did not follow suit in some ethnic minority communities. Instead, gender policies reinforced a rigid sexual division of labor and, because of inadequate amenities, were often primarily geared toward fulfilling economic plans rather than promoting women's liberation. Women were being called upon to be "shock workers" as well as "heroine mothers." In the Muslim regions of the Soviet Union, the unveiling (in Soviet Central Asia known as *hujum,* lit. "onslaught") efforts, although presented as a largely emancipatory program to free women from stiff religious hierarchies, in practice pushed women out of their homes and into the cotton fields. The effects of cotton cultivation (and the heavy use of pesticides and other chemical agents) on women's health were disproportionately disruptive.[119]

## *1950s–1970s*

Khrushchev's Secret Speech (1956) condemned Stalinist terror and reversed or scaled back some of the most repressive policies. As a result, many previously deported groups were permitted to return to their homelands. Khrushchev believed that the nationality issue had largely been solved; as he alleged, "ultimately, the various peoples of the USSR would grow closely together culturally until they blended into a single nation."[120] The attention was placed on forging the new Soviet man – "a supranational, a-national citizen who was an amalgamation of all Soviet peoples."[121]

Khrushchev, and particularly Brezhnev, oversaw a partial return to "indigenization" and the nationality policy practiced in the 1920s. Perhaps as a consequence, the late 1950s were marked by increased Indigenous cadres in many spheres. The institutionalized cadre policy involved appointing a local

---

[119] *Hujum* refers to a broad campaign undertaken by the Soviet government to remove all manifestations of gender inequality within the Union Republics of Central Asia, starting from 1927. See Deniz Kandiyoti, "The Politics of Gender and the Soviet Paradox: Neither Colonized, nor Modern?," *Central Asian Survey* 26, no. 4 (December 2007): 609; Madina Tlostanova, "The Janus-Faced Empire Distorting Orientalist Discourses: Gender, Race and Religion in the Russian/(Post)Soviet Constructions of the 'Orient'," *Worlds and Knowledges Otherwise* 2, no. 2 (Spring 2008): 1–11.

[120] Ronald Grigor Suny, *The Soviet Experiment: Russia, the USSR, and the Successor States* (Oxford University Press, 1998), 411.

[121] Jason A. Roberts, "The Anti-Imperialist Empire: Soviet Nationality Policies under Brezhnev" (PhD diss., West Virginia University, 2014), 63–64.

official to the top position (first secretary) in each republic's Communist Party and the simultaneous appointment of an ethnic Russian to the second position (known informally as the second secretary).[122] Brezhnev was "not inclined to interfere in local affairs as long as they [local Party cadres] maintained stability, paid symbolic fealty, and supplied resources to the central government," which allowed local republic elites "to extract vast spoils from the state and to plow much of this into local patronage networks."[123] In the republics, titular elites were also able to pursue assimilatory policies with respect to the minorities "nested" within the administrative territory.[124] Institutional pluralism developed even within the structures of the Party; the new generation of technocrats was marked by a will to reform and the pace of decentralization quickened to the advantage of the republics.

By and large, although intended as a society of equal citizens, the Soviet policies in the second half of the twentieth century recreated and, in many aspects, reinforced social hierarchies that existed in the imperial period, as outlined below.

1) *Urban versus rural*: By default, the Soviet system favored urban and industrial development, leading it to view traditional agrarian cultures, particularly nomadic societies, as destined for historical oblivion. The impact of Soviet governance on the cultures of smaller and so-called less developed ethnic groups – namely those without industrialization, residing in rural areas, and lacking literacy – was profoundly destructive.[125]

2) *Periphery versus center*: Although Siberia and Central Asia had been much more integrated into the Soviet economic and political system, when compared with the imperial period, different regions and, hence, populations continued to be ranked higher based on their closer proximity to political and cultural centers like Moscow and Leningrad or to the West, as in case of Baltic states in the post-World War II period.

3) *Russian versus non-Russian*: The victory in World War II endowed the Soviet regime with a new popular legitimacy. The emerging consensus had a strong Russo-centrist bias, and the other Soviet republics were included in the global narrative of victory on the condition that they remain

---

[122] Astrid S. Tuminez, "Nationalism, Ethnic Pressures, and the Breakup of the Soviet Union," *Journal of Cold War Studies* 5, no. 4 (Fall 2003): 90.

[123] Hale, *Patronal Politics*, 53.

[124] Krista Goff, *Nested Nationalism: Making and Unmaking Nations in the Soviet Caucasus* (Cornell University Press, 2021).

[125] Yuri Slezkine, *Arctic Mirrors: Russia and the Small Peoples of the North* (Cornell University Press, 1994). On the devastation of Central Asian nomadic societies in the early years of Soviet rule, see Marco Buttino, *La rivoluzione capovolta: L'Asia centrale tra il crollo dell'impero zarista e la formazione dell'Urss* (L'ancora del Mediterraneo, 2003).

subordinate to the Russian-centric narrative.[126] Despite the hybridization of two legitimacies, both Russian and Soviet, Russo-centrism regained momentum after the war: The authorities wanted to monitor the entirety of intellectual and artistic life anew and contributed to rigidifying historical and cultural discourses. The ideology of the "friendship of peoples" placed ethnic Russians in the position of *primus inter pares*, the "elder brother" to other non-Russian communities.[127]

Throughout the Soviet period, the image of the ideal Soviet person – intended as a supranational identity – had become closely identified with Russian culture.[128] Though Russians mostly occupied symbolically important positions, they nonetheless did not live as French colonists in Algeria: Dominant in industry, mining, and construction sites, numerous in many agricultural regions, and in sectors such as teaching and medicine, they mixed with the local populations in local public administrations, and in supposedly national sectors, such as cotton in Central Asia. The situation also differed depending on the republic: In Uzbekistan, Georgia, Armenia, and the Baltic countries, the feeling of "being at home" was less assured and counterbalanced by the stronger assertion of the titular groups' presence in the republic, whereas it was far more certain in Belarus, Ukraine, or Kazakhstan.

4) *Racial hierarchies*: Race was not defined as biological inferiority within the Marxist-Leninist framework. However, the Soviet government embraced an ideology referred to as "state-sponsored evolutionism," which served as the Soviet version of the civilizing mission.[129] This ideology intertwined Marxist notions of historical progression with European anthropological theories centered on cultural evolution. Some groups were regarded as destined for extinction, while others faced persecution due to their perceived "incorrect" ethnic origins and claims to group identity.[130]

---

126 Jonathan Brunstedt, "Elder Brother, Loyal Friend, and the Stalinist Myth of War: Recasting Soviet Ethnic Hierarchy, 1945–1953," *Ab Imperio*, no. 3 (December 2019): 88–116.

127 Jeff Sahadeo, *Voices from the Soviet Edge: Southern Migrants in Leningrad and Moscow* (Cornell University Press, 2019).

128 Mark R. Beissinger, "Soviet Empire as 'Family Resemblance'," *Slavic Review* 65, no. 2 (Summer 2006): 294–303; Ronald Grigor Suny and Terry Martin, eds, *A State of Nations: Empire and Nation-Making in the Age of Lenin and Stalin* (Oxford University Press, 2001); Aleksandr Etkind, Dirk Uffel'mann, and Ilya Kukulin, *Praktiki vnutrennei kolonizatsii v kul'turnoi istorii Rossii* (Novoe literaturnoe obozrenie, 2012); Gulnaz Sharafutdinova, *The Red Mirror: Putin's Leadership and Russia's Insecure Identity* (Oxford University Press, 2020).

129 Hirsch, *Empire of Nations*.

130 Nikolai Zakharov and Ian Law, *The Logics and Legacy of Soviet Racialization: Post-Soviet Racisms* (Palgrave Macmillan, 2017), 1–15; Eric D. Weitz, "Racial Politics without the Concept of Race: Reevaluating Soviet Ethnic and National Purges," *Slavic Review* 61, no. 1 (Spring 2002): 1–29.

Although racism was condemned at the official level, the practices of ethnic essentialization laid the ground for assigning "social and cultural significance" to a "group of people who are recognized as sharing common physical or physiognomic characteristics and/or a common lineage of descent."[131] Ethnic hierarchies defined the rights of groups, and racist views were visible in everyday Soviet life (for instance, in phrases "like a white man," often used humorously but implicitly suggesting the superiority and higher social status of ethnic Russians and Slavs more broadly).[132]

Certain groups were disproportionately affected by racialization policies, with ideas and policies often rooted in Tsarist Russia.[133] Indeed, both in the imperial and Soviet eras, the state sought to modernize groups deemed "backward" and incapable of independent modernization. In Soviet Muslim regions, this led to the successful de-Islamization of public discourse, destroying the means through which Islamic knowledge was created and communicated. Although many other European states have sought to control Islam and Muslims, the uniqueness of the Soviet experience lies in the intensity of this assault, the sustained length of this process, and the way in which it de-modernized Islam as a symbol of national heritage.[134]

### The Soviet Union Administrative Structure

The Soviet Union's ethno-territorial administrative structure fused ethnic identity with hierarchically organized territory. At the top of this hierarchy were the fifteen union republics, named after a "titular" ethnic group (i.e., Kazakh, Ukrainian, Armenian) and which had a comparatively higher degree of autonomy, including greater symbolic representation in the upper chamber of the USSR's parliament (the Supreme Soviet). Nested within the union republics and with less autonomy and representation were *autonomous republics*, and *autonomous provinces* another rung below that.

---

[131] Ian Law, *Racism and Ethnicity: Global Debates, Dilemmas, Directions* (Pearson, 2010), 2–3.

[132] Victor Schnirelman, "Race, Ethnicity, and Cultural Racism in Soviet and Post-Soviet Ideology, Communication, and Practice," in *Oxford Research Encyclopedia of Communication*, https://doi.org/10.1093/acrefore/9780190228613.013.1323.

[133] The Gypsies – not discussed in this section – constituted a group persecuted throughout the Soviet Union and the Eastern bloc. See Brigid O'Keeffe, "The Racialization of Soviet Gypsies: Roma, Nationality Politics, and Socialist Transformation in Stalin's Soviet Union," in *Ideologies of Race: Imperial Russia and the Soviet Union in Global Context*, ed. David Rainbow (McGill-Queen's University Press, 2019), 132–59.

[134] Adeeb Khalid, *Islam after Communism: Religion and Politics in Central Asia* (University of California Press, 2014).

As of 1989, sixteen *autonomous republics* were nested within the Russian Socialist Federative Soviet Republic (RSFSR), with an additional two in Georgia (Abkhazia, Adjara), one in Azerbaijan (Nakhichevan), and one in Uzbekistan (Karakalpakstan). Most ethnic administrative units contained sizeable minority populations.

These borders changed multiple times during the Soviet period, either from the Soviet Union annexing new territory (e.g., occupation of the Baltic states, post-World War II annexation of territories in Eastern Europe to Russia, Ukraine, Belarus), transferring territory from one union republic to another (Crimea in 1954 from Russia to Ukraine), or by changing a territorial unit's position in the administrative hierarchy. Most ethno-nationalist movements in the late Soviet period initially focused on *upgrading* a unit's autonomy in this system rather than on full independence.

Antisemitic propaganda and practices also fueled racial attitudes toward Jews, particularly after World War II. Campaigns against "cosmopolitanism," a new euphemism for antisemitism, continued to grow during the headlong rush of Stalin's last years,[135] which included the arrest of thousands of Party members of Jewish origin accused of bourgeois nationalism; the night of the Murdered Poets (1952), during which thirteen Yiddish poets were killed on Stalin's orders; the closure of the Jewish anti-fascist committee in 1948 and secret trial of Jewish intellectuals in 1952; the so-called "Doctors' plot" (1951–53), which led to the arrest, at Stalin's behest, of several hundreds of doctors and pharmacists of Jewish origin accused of having assassinated Soviet leaders; and the disappearance of information about the Holocaust.[136]

Between the 1970s and the 1980s, racial discourse toward "Blacks," a term that gained popularity in the late 1960s, developed in some segments of Soviet society, sometimes resulting in spontaneous attacks against African (and Asian) students in Moscow and other cities.[137] People from the Caucasus and Central Asia increasingly experienced everyday racism when traveling across Russia,

---

[135] Gennady V. Kostyrchenko, *Out of the Red Shadows: Anti-Semitism in Stalin's Russia* (Prometheus Books, 1995).

[136] Louis Rappaport, *Stalin's War Against the Jews: The Doctors' Plot and the Soviet Solution* (Free Press, 1990); Jonathan Brent and Vladimir Naumov, *Le Dernier crime de Staline: Retour sur le complot des blouses blanches* (Calmann-Lévy, 2006).

[137] Konstantinos Katsakioris, "Afrikanskie studenty v SSSR: Ucheba i politika vo vremia dekolonizatsii, 1960-e gody," in *Sotsial'naia istoriia: Ezhegodnik 2008*, ed. Natal'ia L. Pushkareva (Aleteja, 2009), 221–23; Maxim Matusevich, "Expanding the Boundaries of the Black Atlantic: African Students as Soviet Moderns," *Ab Imperio*, no. 2 (Summer 2012): 325–50.

especially in the big metropoles.[138] The ambivalence and occasional hostility with which Soviet commentators responded to iconic Civil Rights figures, such as Malcolm X and Martin Luther King Jr., revealed the ideological constraints of the system when dealing with non-Marxist movements for racial emancipation in the West.[139]

## Territory

### *1920s–1930s*

Population management in the Soviet Union was closely intertwined with extensive and pervasive control over territories and resources. In its pursuit of rapid economic modernization, Soviet leaders sought to create an alternative to a capitalist economic system, favoring a planned economy with no private ownership. In the early years, the Bolsheviks launched an industrialization program to address the economic challenges inherited from the tsarist regime and strengthen the country's industrial capacity. This capacity was not only essential for safeguarding the Soviet Union's sovereignty but also for competing with capitalist nations on the global stage, as the Bolsheviks sought to pursue the Marxist vision of a global union of proletarian nations.

Broadly speaking, the Soviet culture of territory management promoted the ideology of conquering nature. The Soviet regime often employed revolutionary rhetoric and romanticism, promoting narratives of revolutionary struggle, renewal, and reconstruction to describe human contact with nature. According to the prevailing discourse, nature lacked inherent meaning or rationality; its significance only emerged through the actions of civilized humanity, which bestowed character and purpose upon specific localities through their development and utilization.[140] In that aspect, the Soviet experience shared a similar language with the capitalist West and the idea of an endless exploitation of the natural environment.

---

[138] Kesha Fikes and Alaina Lemon, "African Presence in Former Soviet Spaces," *Annual Review of Anthropology* 31, no. 1 (2002): 507, 515–16; Jeff Sahadeo, "Black Snouts Go Home! Migration and Race in Late Soviet Leningrad and Moscow," *Journal of Modern History* 88, no. 4 (December 2016): 797–826.

[139] Hilary Lynd and Thom Loyd, "Histories of Color: Blackness and Africanness in the Soviet Union," *Slavic Review* 81, no. 2 (Summer 2022): 394–417; Maxim Matusevich, "Soviet Antiracism and Its Discontents: The Cold War Years," in *Alternative Globalizations: Eastern Europe and the Postcolonial World*, ed. James Mark, Artemy Kalinovsky, and Steffi Marung (Indiana University Press, 2020), 229–50.

[140] Alla Bolotova, "Colonization of Nature in the Soviet Union: State Ideology, Public Discourse, and the Experience of Geologists," *Historical Social Research/Historische Sozialforschung* 29, no. 3 (2004): 104–23.

Through the practices of indigenization and collectivization, particularly in Central Asia, Siberia, and further east, the Soviet regime asserted de jure control over lands, disrupting traditional land tenure systems. The exploitation of these lands, resource extraction, and their conversion for agricultural purposes exemplified colonial-style land use and the institutionalization of injustices against Indigenous communities.[141] However, it is worth noting that Soviet colonialism differed significantly from its tsarist predecessor – the Soviet government was not only exploiting these distant regions but also sought to politically and economically integrate local populations into the Soviet Union. In Central Asia, these policies prioritized the production and export of raw materials, primarily cotton, to enhance the Soviet foreign trade balance.

In Siberia, the state utilized the region as a resource frontier and a penal colony. By structuring the regional economy to meet the demands of Soviet industry, the leadership made these regions economically reliant on the rest of the USSR for trade goods and food supplies, preventing them from insulating themselves against "goods shortages" or other trade-related shocks. Cities in Siberia heavily relied on central government subsidies for fuel, food, and transportation. In essence, especially in Central Asia, the transition was made from an "overseas" colony, ruled from a distance by the tsarist government, to an internal colony under the Soviet state. This economic integration into the Soviet Union gave rise to a new, more comprehensive subordinate relationship between the center and the periphery, one that was qualitatively distinct and far-reaching compared with the tsarist era.[142]

### 1950s–1970s

The Soviet economy remained heavily militarized, especially amid increasing tensions with the United States (since 1945) and China (after 1960), which had some substantial structural implications (e.g., some civilian industries falling behind). But this period also involved concrete attempts to implement the socialist welfare system. Under Khrushchev, social security coverage was expanded to encompass most workers and their dependents (although collective farm workers remained excluded). Pensions doubled, and disability and survivor allowances saw substantial increases. Moreover, efforts were undertaken to reduce disparities in benefits.[143] Between 1956 and 1970, an

---

[141] Julian Agyeman and Yelena Ogneva-Himmelberger, eds, *Environmental Justice and Sustainability in the Former Soviet Union* (MIT Press, 2009).

[142] Benjamin Loring, "'Colonizers with Party Cards': Soviet Internal Colonialism in Central Asia, 1917–39," *Kritika: Explorations in Russian and Eurasian History* 15, no. 1 (Winter 2014): 77–102.

[143] Gordon B. Smith, *Soviet Politics: Continuity and Contradiction* (Palgrave, 1988), 265.

impressive 34.2 million housing units were constructed in the USSR to accommodate over half of the entire population of the Soviet Union. A significant number of single-family apartments were built with the aim of eliminating much-dreaded communal apartments.[144] The healthcare sector received a substantial portion of the funds allocated for social services. In 1964, the mortality rate for the Soviet population was lower than that in the United States and many other developed Western nations.[145]

The most important episode of the new internal colonial policy in this period was the agricultural development of Virgin Lands (1954–61). More specifically, efforts were aimed at turning lands in Central Asia into fertile ground for cotton and, to a lesser extent, rice production; the construction of the Bratsk hydro-electric power station (1954–67); and the Baikal-Amur Mainline (1972–84), designed to provide better and more expedient trade corridors through Eastern Siberia and further east, doubling the amount of rail traffic that could reach Pacific ports.[146] Invasive Soviet irrigation projects during the 1960s–1980s allowed cotton production to almost double, turning the Soviet Union into a producer of one-quarter of the world's cotton. This output, however, quickly declined, not least because of serious environmental problems resulting from the process.

In a framework where the government held manufacturing authority and production targets took precedence, environmental considerations were consistently relegated beneath industrial objectives. Pervasive pollution, excessive resource consumption, and overall environmental degradation followed.[147] The Aral Sea, previously the fourth-largest freshwater expanse globally, underwent a reduction to just one-third of its original size due to extended irrigation-driven drainage.

In the context of the arms and space race, the Soviet Union faced devastating human-caused disasters and environmental damage, which impacted millions of people. For example, nuclear missile testing in the Semipalatinsk region exposed more than one million people to radiation.[148] In a more well-known event, the Chernobyl nuclear power plant explosion in 1986 had catastrophic consequences

---

[144] Ibid., 252.    [145] Ibid., 259.

[146] Christopher J. Ward, *Brezhnev's Folly: The Building of BAM and Late Soviet Socialism* (University of Pittsburgh Press, 2009).

[147] D. J. Peterson, *Troubled Lands: The Legacy of Soviet Environmental Destruction* (Westview Press, 1993).

[148] The Parliament of the Republic of Kazakhstan, "Spravka po voprosu 'Ob okhrane zdorov'ia i sotsial'noi zashchite naseleniia, prozhivaiushchego v zone vliianiia byvshego Semipalatinskogo iadernogo poligona'," June 24, 2005, https://online.zakon.kz/Document/?doc_id=30026965& pos=2;-34#pos=2;-34; Togzhan Kassenova, *Atomic Steppe: How Kazakhstan Gave Up the Bomb* (Stanford University Press, 2022).

for human health and the environment in vast territories, exposing hundreds of thousands to nuclear radiation.

## Conclusion

In examining the Soviet experiment as an example of colonial modernity, one needs to look at the intersection of two contextual frameworks: the legacy of its predecessor, Tsarist Russia, and the wider context of European modernity. This dual perspective helps explain the Soviet Union's development, particularly in how it addressed the "nationalities question" inherited from the Tsarist Empire.

The Bolsheviks dealt with many institutional structures, organizational units, and cultural policies passed down from Tsarist Russia. These elements played a significant role in shaping the early trajectory of the Soviet state, which struggled to manage the relationship between the majority, politically and culturally dominant Russian nation, and non-Russian ethnic groups, many of which had aspirations to establish independent states. Both the tsarist and Soviet regimes constructed ethnic and national categories with profound political implications, categorizing citizens and subjecting them to nationality-based policies. Despite the federal structure and promises of autonomy for non-Russian peoples, the Soviet Union largely retained the imperial models in a center–periphery relationship and maintained the superiority of the Russian culture above minority cultures.

At the same time, Soviet socialism was a complex and multifaceted response to the challenges and aspirations of European modernity. The Soviet state embarked on a uniquely large-scale radical transformation and reorganization of its population. In doing so, it pursued the ideals of rational and productive societal organization, emphasized scientific knowledge, and applied an array of social science and biosocial approaches to reorder society on a rational basis – sharing a lot of philosophical principles with Western modernity.

In its modality, this kind of population management was not unique to the USSR but reflected broader Western trends: European nations at the time shared a common goal of efficiently managing and structuring their societies, treating the population as a resource to be mobilized and utilized for maximum productivity. While the specter of mass warfare, especially in the first half of the twentieth century, strongly influenced these policies, they trace their roots to broader modern developments such as industrialization, urbanization, imperialism, and the influence of social Darwinism.[149]

---

[149] David L. Hoffmann, "European Modernity and Soviet Socialism," in *Russian Modernity: Politics, Knowledge, Practices*, ed. David Hoffmann and Yanni Kotsonis (Palgrave Macmillan UK, 2000), 245–60.

However, while noble in its idealistic pursuit of a harmonious social order, the Soviet leadership – especially under Stalin – was exceptionally brutal and violent in applying coercive measures, such as imprisonment, torture, deportation, and ethnic cleansing, to reshape and discipline its populace. Many non-Russian communities were disproportionately affected by intersecting anti-religion, sedentarization, collectivization, and gender policies. As the postmodern era unfolded, it became evident that the government's extensive intervention in people's lives had not succeeded in creating a socialist utopia; the limitations of a planned economy became a serious hindrance to progress; and foreign policy, which once seemed to usher forward the global solidarity movement, led to long and exhausting proxy conflicts.

## 3 Post-Socialist Transition: Decolonization and Recolonization

The collapse of the Soviet Union in 1991 is commonly regarded as a major moment in the history of decolonization, as fifteen formerly Soviet states became independent. International recognition of Armenia, Azerbaijan, Belarus, Estonia, Georgia, Kazakhstan, Kyrgyzstan, Latvia, Lithuania, Moldova, Russia, Tajikistan, Turkmenistan, Ukraine, and Uzbekistan as sovereign states has generally been interpreted as the culmination of these countries' struggle for independence under both the tsarist and Soviet regimes. This reading of historical events, however, tends to blend top–down decisions made in the late 1980s and early 1990s with long-term grassroots struggles for autonomy and/or independence, while the emphasis on political independence glosses over new forms of dependence that emerged between the center (Moscow) and the periphery (now independent countries) in late 1991.

Following the breakup of the USSR, Russia found itself in an ambivalent status of being both one of the countries struggling to free itself from the Soviet framework *and* the historical successor of the Soviet Union. It had to deal with the pressure and tensions of critically reevaluating its history from within while expressing neocolonial ambitions in its so-called near abroad.[150] Although Russia's elites have profited from integration into the West-oriented (and fossil-fuel-dependent) market economy, the Kremlin has ideologically insisted on following a different path – one that is increasingly defined as an alternative to the West. Over the last few decades, the Russian state has gradually but successfully adopted postcolonial language centered around a critique of liberalism, (neo)colonial relations, and a universalist understanding of human rights

---

[150] Gerard Toal, *Near Abroad: Putin, the West, and the Contest over Ukraine and the Caucasus* (Oxford University Press, 2019).

and values, endorsing, thereby, not a leftist emancipatory project, but a form of right-wing post-colonial nationalism.[151]

## *Perestroika*: Top–Down and Bottom–Up Transformations

Upon assuming the General Secretary position in 1985, Mikhail Gorbachev recognized the urgent need for economic reforms to revive the failing Soviet command economy strained by excessive military spending. He initiated *perestroika* ("re-building") reforms in 1987–88 to shift from a command economy to a mixed and eventually market-based economy. At the same time, Gorbachev – who belonged to the generation of *shestedesiatniki* (people of the 1960s),[152] young adults during Khruschev's thaw and post-Stalin liberalization – advocated for the second pillar of his reform program: opening and democratizing the social system and the state's relationship with the public (*glasnost'*). These reforms were revolutionary in nature, and they were unquestionably supported by a significant share of Soviet society. However, factors beyond Gorbachev's control, such as the speed of reforms and dissent among party leadership, made implementing these changes immensely challenging.

By 1989, communist power structures in the USSR had largely dissolved without viable alternatives in place.[153] On the domestic economic front, the country was in serious foreign debt, and people's savings had sharply declined in value, creating economic problems for the next generation of politicians to deal with. Gorbachev's foreign policy aimed to improve relations with the West and China, withdrawing Soviet influence from developing countries,[154] negotiating an end to the Cold War, and envisioning the USSR as part of a new global community. His "liberation" of Central European countries was in many ways a symbolic move; by fostering the democratization of socialist countries in Eastern Europe, Moscow signaled its desire for rapprochement with the West and sought to reinsert the Soviet Union into Europe.

Gorbachev's concessions in Europe and in developing countries did not translate to dismantling the Soviet Union. On the contrary, historical evidence suggests that while granting rights to Western neighbors, the Soviet leader worked to resist independence movements within the Soviet Union. In December 1986, the authorities harshly suppressed peaceful demonstrations

---

[151] Dirk Uffelmann, "Postcolonial Theory as Post-Colonial Nationalism," in *Postcolonialism Cross-Examined*, ed. Monika Albrecht (Routledge, 2019), 135–52.

[152] Vladimir Gel'man and Dmitrii Travin, "'Zagoguliny' rossiiskoi modernizatsii: smena pokolenii i traektorii reform," *Neprikosnovennyi zapas*, no. 4 (2013): 14–38.

[153] Vladislav M. Zubok, *Collapse: The Fall of the Soviet Union* (Yale University Press, 2021).

[154] Robert G. Patman, "Reagan, Gorbachev and the Emergence of 'New Political Thinking'," *Review of International Studies* 25, no. 4 (1999): 577–601.

in Kazakhstan (the *Jeltoqsan* events). In 1989, thousands of Soviet troops were sent to Uzbekistan, Georgia and, in January 1990, to restore order in Baku, the capital of Azerbaijan. In January 1991, after all three Baltic republics had declared independence from the USSR – pronounced illegal by Moscow – the Soviet military tried to dismantle barricades erected in Riga and Vilnius, leading to dozens of deaths on the Baltic side.

## The Collapse of the Soviet Union and Subsequent Decolonization

Gorbachev's efforts to secure national unity through a new union treaty were disrupted by the conservative-led coup of August 1991. Russia, under Yeltsin's leadership, played a pivotal role in seizing the opportunity of political chaos and suspending the Russian Communist Party. In December 1991, the Soviet Union dissolved after Ukraine, Russia, and Belarus signed the Belovezha Accords.[155] Two weeks later, the three signatories, as well as eight additional former Soviet republics signed the Alma-Ata Protocols, formally establishing the Commonwealth of Independent States (CIS).

Following the dissolution of the Soviet Union in 1991, all of the newly independent countries adopted the discourse of postcolonial liberation; notably, however, the communist elites remained in power in several of them. In Russia this paradox was even more stark, in part owing to the fact that Moscow inherited significant Soviet institutional legacies, importantly becoming its legal successor and taking up its seat at the United Nations Security Council (UNSC).[156] For instance, while the Belovezha Accords declared that the USSR ceased to exist as a subject of international law, Yeltsin's subsequent letter to the United Nations claimed that Russia was "continuing" the Soviet Union's membership.[157] While not predetermined, this arrangement was in many ways the least problematic outcome at the time: the other four permanent members of the UNSC were anxious to maintain institutional continuity, while the United States sought to avoid a "Yugoslavia with nukes," which required both the support and stability of Moscow to achieve. As for the leaders of the newly independent states, endorsing this succession as part of the Alma-Ata Protocols was understood as a way of ensuring the dissolution of the Soviet Union, while Russia becoming its successor would also free the other leaders of assuming part of the Soviet Union's outstanding financial obligations.[158]

---

[155] Zbigniew Brzezinski and Paige Sullivan, eds, *Russia and the Commonwealth of Independent States: Documents, Data, and Analysis* (M. E. Sharpe, 1997), 41.

[156] Mark Kramer, "The Soviet Legacy in Russian Foreign Policy," *Political Science Quarterly* 134, no. 4 (2019): 585–609.

[157] Michael P. Scharf, "Musical Chairs: The Dissolution of States and Membership in the United Nations," *Cornell International Law Journal* 28, no. 1 (1995): 30–69.

[158] Serhii Plokhy, *The Last Empire: The Final Days of the Soviet Union* (Basic Books, 2014), 363.

Importantly, the Soviet collapse did not primarily stem from popular mobilization for liberation or anticolonial action, except in the Baltic states and to a lesser extent in Ukraine and Georgia (though grassroots mobilization of minority language advocates, ecological activists, and Islamic community leaders existed also in Central Asia and Russia). Rather, the decentralization process was initiated by the central authorities in Moscow, due to mounting difficulties in sustaining the union of the republics amid several economic, political, and social crises. Gorbachev even encouraged proclamations of sovereignty by autonomous regions within the Soviet republics – though primarily as a tit-for-tat move in response to Russia's own assertion of its sovereignty. In response, Yeltsin famously urged the autonomous regions to take as much sovereignty as they could "swallow."[159]

Once the decentralization process began, the center could not quell the demands for independence and sovereignty from the periphery, including the national entities within Russia itself. The Soviet nationalities policy effectively created nation-states "in embryo." During *perestroika*, Moscow-led reforms provided ethnic elites with potent tools with which to assert themselves against the central authority. These newly formed entities adopted a Euro-centric nation-state model, aligning with the internationally recognized norm established in the 1960s for end-of-empire scenarios. This norm, governed by the principle of *uti possidetis jure*, upholds existing administrative boundaries established by colonial powers; new countries were to follow the exact boundaries of their Soviet republics, yet several territorial conflicts still emerged.[160]

## Neoliberal Economic Reforms

Although de jure politically independent from the former metropole, the post-Soviet and post-socialist countries quickly found themselves involved in new – yet still unequal and often exploitative – relations. A significant body of scholarship has expressed a critique of how, during the post-socialist "transition" – imagined as a linear and fairly straightforward move toward both democracy and market-based capitalism – Central and Eastern European countries were subjected to neocolonialist practices amid their incorporation into global markets, which favored the economic gains of elites over the social protection of the masses.[161]

---

[159] Ben Fowkes, *The Disintegration of the Soviet Union: A Study in the Rise and Triumph of Nationalism* (Springer, 1997), 180.

[160] James Hughes, "Chechnya: The Causes of a Protracted Post-Soviet Conflict," *Civil Wars* 4, no. 4 (2001): 15.

[161] Veronika Pehe and Joanna Wawrzyniak, eds, *Remembering the Neoliberal Turn: Economic Change and Collective Memory in Eastern Europe after 1989* (Routledge, 2023); Kristen Rogheh Ghodsee and Mitchell Alexander Orenstein, *Taking Stock of Shock: Social Consequences of the 1989 Revolutions* (Oxford University Press, 2021).

Indeed, the dissolution of the Soviet Union occurred concurrently with the Western world's pivot toward neoliberalism. Neoliberal ideas spread at a rapid pace not only because they promised economic revitalization to faltering economies but also because they were said to bring certain political advantages. In Russia, which was simultaneously attempting to transition to both democracy *and* market-based capitalism,[162] proponents of neoliberal reforms argued that it was important to move quickly while society was in a state of disarray and before representatives of the previous regime could regroup and reverse the transition. This "shock therapy" eventually led the former Soviet elites to convert to proponents of a market economy. The transition came at an extremely high cost to the population, and the idea of liberal competitive capitalism was never truly actualized. The results of the "shock therapy" were devastating for ordinary Russian citizens, who experienced faltering incomes, food supply shortages, and serious economic crises, which collectively came to be referred to as 1990s transition trauma. In the long run, the economic reforms of the 1990s created the conditions for the authoritarian regime that solidified itself under the presidency of Vladimir Putin.[163]

DEMOGRAPHICS AND ADMINISTRATIVE STRUCTURE OF THE RUSSIAN FEDERATION

Russia inherited many aspects of the previous Soviet ethno-federal structure. Of Russia's eighty-three administrative units, twenty-seven originate directly from the ethnic specificity of their populations, twenty-one of which are *republics*, consisting of the sixteen *autonomous republics* that existed in the Soviet Union in 1989 plus five (the splitting of the Chechen-Ingush *autonomous republic* into Chechnya and Ingushetia, plus four former *autonomous provinces*). Some of these regions have a single "titular" ethnic group (e.g., Tatarstan, Buryatia, Sakha (Yakutia)), while others have two (Khanty-Mansi, Kabardino-Balkaria, Karachay-Cherkessia) or more (i.e., Dagestan, with thirteen recognized constitutive ethnic groups).

These borders, too, have shifted over time. Under Putin there have been several mentions of the need to eliminate administrative differences between regions. This process has so far only been piecemeal – the incorporation of several small Siberian autonomous districts (Nenets, Khanti-Mansi, Yamalo-Nenets, as well as two Buryat districts) into neighboring

---

[162] Anders Aslund, "Why Market Reform Succeeded and Democracy Failed in Russia," *Social Research* 75, no. 4 (2009): 1–28.

[163] Sharafutdinova, *The Red Mirror*.

regions between 2004 and 2008 generated grassroots resistance. Moreover, regions can, per Article 67 of the Russian Constitution, mutually agree to exchange territory, though this, too, has aroused grassroots resistance, such as the 2018 land swap between Chechnya and Ingushetia, which sparked mass protests in Ingushetia and saw its leader resign shortly after.

Altogether, about fifty ethnic groups benefit from public policies that preserve, at least on paper, their vernacular language and ethnic culture in the local education system, as well as giving titular representatives priority access to high positions in local government.

Nonethnic Russian citizens represent around 20 percent of the population. These include around seventeen million Muslims, living predominantly in the Volga region (Tatarstan, Bashkortostan) and the North Caucasus. To this one can add several Finno-Ugric populations in European Russia and peoples of Siberia and the Far North, many of which have been linguistically heavily Russified. Ethnic Ukrainian and Belarusian minorities have historically been sizeable, although the number self-identifying as such has dramatically decreased, both due to intermarriage and Russification as well as geopolitical tensions.

We do not include here the five administrative units that Russia annexed from Ukraine (Autonomous Republic of Crimea, together with Donetsk, Luhansk, Kherson and Zaporizhzhia Oblasts).

## Russia's Decentralization and Recentralization

In the 1990s, multiple regions of Russia acquired a significant degree of autonomy, and the state adopted a wide variety of approaches to political, economic, and cultural reform. This period of pluralism entailed debate over the range of possible relational dynamics between the federal center and the regions. However, in the 2000s, a period of authoritarian centralization under Putin began; the state put checks and limits on regional autonomy, ultimately undoing most aspects of regional sovereignty and taking an increasingly centralizing and repressive line toward matters of regional sovereignty and regional identity.

### *Varying Degrees of Subnational Autonomy*

It is worth highlighting just how varied identity and autonomy were in Russia in the 1990s, when the new state could be considered an "asymmetric federation."[164] Local political elites engaged in state- and nation-building policies at the local level, creating state-like institutions (e.g., presidencies, constitutions, flags), crafting regional educational policies around local history and languages, providing public goods and services, and even engaging in international diplomacy (Tatarstan, for example, opened sixteen foreign missions in the 1990s).[165] Moscow's relations with the republics were regulated by bilateral treaties; the first such treaty was made with Tatarstan in 1994, but this was followed by another forty-five by 1998.[166] Regional governors also had a direct role in federal policy, capable of taking seats in the upper house (Federation Council) until 2000.

There were also significant variations in the strength and intensity of identity-based demands.[167] Regions like Tatarstan and Bashkortostan in the Volga region, Sakha (Yakutia) and Tuva in Siberia, and the republics of the North Caucasus housed significant bottom–up ethnic mobilization, which – in terms of the number and intensity of protests – surpassed those in many of the union republics.[168] Some ethnic republics, such as Udmurtia and Komi, had mild regionalist movements, and not all regionalisms were ethnic in nature; majority-Russian regions like Sverdlovsk Oblast (Ural Republic) also developed autonomist movements.[169] In one notable case, Chechnya pursued independence, but Moscow intervened militarily under both Yeltsin (First Chechen War, 1994–96) and Putin (Second Chechen War, 1999–2009), echoing previous colonial wars.[170]

These demands were articulated at the grassroots level in various ways. First, autonomy movements emerged from Soviet-era cultural intelligentsia (e.g., scholars, teachers, artists, architects), so the liberalization of the late Soviet period and early 1990s provided opportunities to rethink history and identity through scholarship, art, architecture, etc., and these opportunities have persisted to the present day (albeit under far more restrictive conditions).[171] Regional presses and publishers proliferated, and, in some regions, this cultural

---

[164] Bill Bowring, "The Russian Constitutional System: Complexity and Asymmetry," in *Asymmetric Autonomy and the Settlement of Ethnic Conflicts*, ed. Marc Weller and Katherine Nobbs (Pennsylvania University Press, 2011), 48–74.

[165] Gulnaz Sharafutdinova, "Paradiplomacy in the Russian Regions: Tatarstan's Search for Statehood," *Europe-Asia Studies* 55, no. 4 (2003): 616.

[166] Cameron Ross, *Federalism and Democratisation in Russia* (Manchester University Press, 2003), 41–44.

[167] Adam Charles Lenton, "Echoes of Empire: Subnationalism and Political Development in the Russian Federation" (PhD diss., George Washington University, 2023).

[168] Beissinger, *Nationalist Mobilization*; Gorenburg, *Minority Ethnic Mobilization*; Elise Giuliano, *Constructing Grievance: Ethnic Nationalism in Russia's Republics* (Cornell University Press, 2017).

[169] Herrera, *Imagined Economies.*     [170] Hughes, "Chechnya," 14.

[171] Gorenburg, *Minority Ethnic Mobilization.*

production was supported and patronized by the local elites. This phenomenon was explicitly understood by many as a manifestation of "decolonization."[172]

Second, people began to reengage with religion as an element of identity that was often complementary to broader decolonial aims of reevaluating groups' historical experiences under Russian rule. Both individuals and regional governments representing ethnic minorities promoted the revival of Islam,[173] Buddhism, or Tengrism.[174] Meanwhile, there were movements among Russian Orthodox minorities that attempted to rediscover and promote pre-Orthodox religious traditions such as paganism, although this was quite marginal except in Mari El.[175]

### Authoritarian Centralization under Putin

Center–region relations would change fundamentally under Putin, with greater authoritarian centralization from Moscow limiting regional sovereignty and repressing ethnic and other regionalist movements. During his first term (2000–04), Putin constrained regional autonomy through several measures, including the creation of seven regional federal districts overseeing the regions, the reformation of the Federation Council, the ability for the president to dismiss regional governors, and recentralization of tax authority – making the regions more dependent on the Kremlin.[176] Bilateral treaties were adjusted to comply with federal legislation, while laws were subject to revision in the Russian Federation Constitution Court rather than in the regions themselves.[177]

As late as 2017, Moscow was still rolling back regional autonomy in language education: republic-level governments were no longer permitted to require schoolchildren to study the local republic's co-official language. The final remaining bilateral treaty between the center and the regions – which, once again, was with Tatarstan – expired in 2017, when Moscow declined to replace

---

172 Katherine E. Graney, "Education Reform in Tatarstan and Bashkortostan: Sovereignty Projects in Post-Soviet Russia," *Europe-Asia Studies* 51, no. 4 (June 1999): 614.

173 Gulnaz Sibgatullina, "The Muftis and the Myths: Constructing the Russian 'Church for Islam'," *Problems of Post-Communism* (2023), DOI: 10.1080/10758216.2023.2185899.

174 Elza-Bair Guchinova, *The Kalmyks* (Routledge, 2006), 166; Edward C. Holland, "Competing Interpretations of Buddhism's Revival in the Russian Republic of Kalmykia," *Europe-Asia Studies* 67, no. 6 (2015): 961; Marlène Laruelle, "Religious Revival, Nationalism and the 'Invention of Tradition': Political Tengrism in Central Asia and Tatarstan," *Central Asian Survey* 26, no. 2 (June 1, 2007): 203–16.

175 Victor A. Shnirel'man, *Neoiazychestvo i natsionalizm (vostochnoevropeiskii region)* (Institut etnologii i antropologii RAN, 1998), 22; Olessia P. Vovina, "Building the Road to the Temple: Religion and National Revival in the Chuvash Republic," *Nationalities Papers* 28, no. 4 (December 1, 2000): 695–706.

176 Ross, *Federalism and Democratisation.*

177 Donna Bahry, "The New Federalism and the Paradoxes of Regional Sovereignty in Russia," *Comparative Politics* 37, no. 2 (2005): 140; Giuliano, *Constructing Grievance,* 122–23.

it with a new one. Authoritarian centralization was accompanied by the starker repression of activists, including members of various ethnic and religious movements who had risen to prominence during the 1990s. While many regions had previously worked to marginalize such movements, this trend accelerated in the 2000s and 2010s through federal support, forcing many local leaders to emigrate.

What remains of institutional decentralization? While decentralization claims are not openly articulated in present-day Russia as they were in the 1990s, there are three spheres in which we can identify symbolic or latent decentralizing tendencies that may still arise. First, political networks remain quite powerful, such as in Chechnya and in Tatarstan; more generally, representatives of titular ethnic groups retain particularly substantial political power in several republics, including at the executive level.[178] Second, as the market economy has developed, a space for cultural nationalism has emerged in the form of "ethnic" goods and services.[179] Third, and relatedly, regional governments have continued to sponsor and promote local cultures even as decentralization as a political goal is now perceived to be subversive, demonstrating that the symbolic basis for claims to decentralization has not disappeared completely.[180]

## Russia's Post-Imperial Projection at Home and Abroad

In its attempt to build a new societal consensus in support of the political status quo, the Russian regime has gradually rehabilitated many elements of its tsarist and Soviet past. It has constructed multiple narratives to justify Russia's uniqueness, all associated, in the Kremlin's mind, with the regime's quest for legitimacy. They are all connected to the idea of Russia as a distinct civilization, sharing features with Europe and sometimes Asia (depending on the specific form of the narrative) but nonetheless always unique.[181]

This official civilizationist narrative relies heavily on a culturalist and primordialist vision of national identity shaped by history and religion, in which individuals have limited agency. It houses a conservative political philosophy that believes in the need to respect order and traditions and to avoid rapid changes, which are framed as bearers of chaos. Over the years, the state

---

[178] Petr Panov, "In Search of Inter-Ethnic Balance: Ethnic Composition and Informal Power-Sharing in Russian National Republics," *European Politics and Society* 17, no. 3 (July 2, 2016): 353–72.

[179] Guzel Yusupova, "Cultural Nationalism and Everyday Resistance in an Illiberal Nationalising State: Ethnic Minority Nationalism in Russia," *Nations and Nationalism* 24, no. 3 (2018): 624–47.

[180] Adam Lenton, "Office Politics: Tatarstan's Presidency and the Symbolic Politics of Regionalism," *Russian Politics* 6, no. 3 (2021): 301–29.

[181] Andrei Tsygankov, "Crafting the State-Civilization: Vladimir Putin's Turn to Distinct Values," *Problems of Post-Communism* 63, no. 3 (April 2016): 146–58.

has projected Russia as a *katekhon*, a withholder or civilizational shield providing the world with spiritual guidance and light amid the chaos and secularization of Western-led liberalism.[182] While officially recognizing multiple religions and ethnic diversity in the country, the Orthodox Church and ethnic Russians hold a primary status, echoing historical hierarchies of dominance.[183]

Another aspect of persistent imperial hierarchies can be found in the rise of xenophobia toward labor migrants (the Russian language even crafted a neologism that can be translated as "migrantophobia"). Thanks to its economic boom, late Soviet and post-Soviet Russia indeed became a key destination for labor migrations from the southern republics of its periphery, namely Tajikistan, Uzbekistan, Kyrgyzstan, Azerbaijan, and Armenia, with substantial migratory flows also coming from Moldova and Ukraine.[184] As in Europe, migrants are accused of stealing jobs from the ethnic core, presenting health-related dangers, being connected to underground criminality, and disturbing established cultural norms.[185] As Sergei Abashin acutely noted, this reflects "a postimperial phenomenon," as "migration reaffirms the division of labor between the former 'center' and the former 'periphery,' their hierarchy and interdependence, despite the rhetoric of sharp repulsion."[186]

Russia's imperial legacy also emerges in a particularly stunning way via the regime's projection of power and self-representation. Russia's spatiality is directly connected to a geopolitical imagination in which imperial legacy dominates.[187] The most widespread concept is likely the notion of Eurasia, which presents Russia as the central actor, the pivotal culture and state of the Eurasian continent. Eurasianism thus appears as the most direct discursive continuation of the notion of the Soviet friendship of peoples, as it assumes a shared destiny for all nations in Eurasia, including the constitutive nations of Russia itself. It relies on an intellectual genealogy that can be traced back to Russian interwar émigré culture, and it benefits from several intellectual or para-intellectual voices that are well represented in Russian media as well as an

---

[182] Maria Engström, "Contemporary Russian Messianism and New Russian Foreign Policy," *Contemporary Security Policy* 35, no. 3 (2014): 356–79.

[183] Alicja Curanović, "Russia's Mission in the World: The Perspective of the Russian Orthodox Church," *Problems of Post-Communism* 66, no. 4 (2019): 253–67.

[184] Jeff Sahadeo, *Voices from the Soviet Edge: Southern Migrants in Leningrad and Moscow* (Cornell University Press, 2019).

[185] Yoshiko M. Herrera and Nicole M. Butkovich Kraus, "Pride versus Prejudice: Ethnicity, National Identity, and Xenophobia in Russia," *Comparative Politics* 48, no. 3 (2016): 293–315.

[186] Sergei Abashin, "Migration from Central Asia to Russia in the New Model of World Order," *Russian Politics and Law* 52, no. 6 (2014): 15–16.

[187] Franck Billé, "Auratic Geographies: Buffers, Backyards, Entanglements," *Geopolitics* 29, no. 3 (2024): 1004–26.

official status, which was instituted when Putin aspired to build a Eurasian Union once he returned to power in 2012.[188]

Another component of the civilizational repertoire is the notion of the Russian World, which encapsulates the idea of Russians as a divided nation with parts of its cultural body beyond the borders of the Federation. Depending on its reading, this notion combines ethno-nationalism, imperialism, and isolationism in a paradoxical way as well as cultural expansion and the projection of soft power.[189] This notion has been used prominently in discourse on Ukraine to justify the annexation of Crimea, support for Donbas secessionism, the dream of a *Novorossiya* ("New Russia") in southeastern Ukraine, and, more recently, the full-scale invasion of Ukraine and the annexation of four of its administrative regions in September 2022.

The notions of both Eurasia and the Russian World entail nuances that are important to our discussion here. Eurasia represents a neocolonial view of spheres of influence as the "business-as-usual" relationship between a former colonial center and its former colonies. In this way, it is similar to the notion of Françafrique, where shared cultural elements such as language, elite-level political ties, military support for authoritarian regimes, labor migration, and economic dominance encapsulate continuities of the colonial relationship between France and French-speaking Africa. The Russian World represents a neo-imperial and ethnic view of Russia: the dismemberment of the imperial territory was accepted as a *fait établi* if the spheres of influence were kept; however, if they were challenged, as with Ukraine's will to shift geopolitically away from Russia, then dismemberment was denounced and a mechanism of rebuilding the destroyed "triune" (the supposed unity of Russians, Ukrainians, and Belarusians) of the imperial past was launched.[190]

## The Polysemy of Grassroots Decolonization Claims

While Russian authorities were reframing old imperial and colonial themes into state rhetoric, civil society actors developed their own grassroots practices

---

188 E.g., Marlene Laruelle, *Russian Eurasianism: An Ideology of Empire* (Woodrow Wilson Press/ Johns Hopkins University Press, 2008); Sergey Glebov, *From Empire to Eurasia: Politics, Scholarship, and Ideology in Russian Eurasianism, 1920s–1930s* (Cornell University Press, 2017); Aliaksei Kazharski, *Eurasian Integration and the Russian World: Regionalism as an Identitary Enterprise* (Central European University Press, 2019).

189 Mikhail Suslov, "'Russian World' Concept: Post-Soviet Geopolitical Ideology and the Logic of 'Spheres of Influence'," *Geopolitics* 23, no. 2 (February 2018): 330–53; Marlene Laruelle, "The 'Russian World': Russia's Soft Power and Geopolitical Imagination," *Center for Global Interests Papers* (May 2015), www.ponarseurasia.org/the-russian-world-russia-s-soft-power-and-geopolitical-imagination/.

190 Aleksei Miller, "Talking Politics: Vladimir Putin's Narrative on Contemporary History (2019– 2022)," *Russia in Global Affairs* 21, no. 2 (2023), https://eng.globalaffairs.ru/articles/putins-narrative/.

involving the critical reevaluation of one's national identity, historical perspective, and position within existing center–periphery relations.

These practices were nothing new, having already emerged during the Soviet era, particularly following Khruschev's thaw in the 1960s, and enjoyed some spaces of freedom in the 1970s. Ilya Kukulin, one of the early analysts of such practices in the literature, characterizes this informal cultural movement as "post-colonial," as the "affirmative action empire" that existed within the Soviet Union during the 1920s and early 1930s framed the national minorities as "already decolonized" communities. The authors analyzed by Kukulin, among others, show critical engagement with the Soviet discourse of "internal colonization" (including both the "exploitative" and "acculturation" facets) and the tangible consequences of coerced modernization across social, political, and ecological dimensions before the 1991 collapse.

Publications such as Kyrgyz writer Chingiz Aitmatov's *The Day Lasts More Than a Hundred Years* in 1980,[191] marked a significant turning point at which bilingual writers from ethnic minority groups began engaging in a critical reassessment of Soviet culture. Their work prompted a critique of cultural essentialism and Soviet modernity, colonial, or authoritarian governance models, and cultural divisions, appropriations, and transformations instigated by colonial encounters. Particularly noteworthy in this context were the contributions of the Riga and Fergana poetry schools. It wasn't until the 2000s, however, that such post-colonial reflection began to gain move visibility within Russia itself.[192]

The conflicts in Chechnya and, more recently, the Russia–Ukraine War have served as catalysts in shaping bottom–up critiques of centralized institutions and practices in Russia, as well as of what has been perceived as colonial legacies. These critiques have highlighted various social and political issues, exposing simultaneously the complexities involved in addressing them.[193]

Recent activism has predominantly focused on *rethinking dominant historical narratives*, especially on reclaiming the memories of those marginalized or omitted from standardized Russian history books. In this context, film emerged as a significant medium in the 2000s and particularly in the 2010s, serving as an experimental space for exploring traumatic historical events. These include the famines of the 1930s, the generational conflicts, the

---

[191] Chengiz Aitmatov, John French, trans., *The Day Lasts More than a Hundred Years* (Indiana University Press, 1983).

[192] Ilya Kukulin, "'Vnutrenniaia postkolonizatsii': formirovanie postkolonial'nogo soznaniia v russkoi literature 1970–2000 godov," *Politicheskaia kontseptologia* 2 (2013): 149–85; Kirill Korchagin, "'Kogda my zamenim svoi mir … ': ferganskaia poeticheskaya shkola v poiskakh postkolonial'nogo sub 'ekta'," *Novoe literaturnoe obozrenie* 144 (2017): 448–70.

[193] The authors express their gratitude to Stas Shärifullá (@hmot.club), who kindly shared his thoughts on the topic.

environmental degradation during the Soviet period, and the resurgence of religion as a mechanism of female oppression.[194] Likewise, literature and contemporary art have become arenas for experimentation. The art scene, in particular, exemplifies the transnational nature of the contemporary decolonial movement across former Soviet states, which scholar Madina Tlostanova characterizes as "post-Soviet decolonial art."[195]

The contemporary focus on culture and the transformation of dominant epistemologies and knowledge systems have been defining features primarily of a "younger" generation of activists, whose formative years unfolded in the 1980s and 1990s. This generation often had access to and engaged with ongoing decolonial debates in the West. Within this context, a question arises, especially in building relations with the "older" generation of ethnic minority activists (many of whom have already been active in the nationalist movements of the 1990s): Must decolonial action necessarily be political, aimed at political emancipation, often understood as the political independence of non-Russian subjects within the Russian Federation? While a segment of decolonial activism advocates for the de-federalization of Russia (as discussed in the next section), some critics argue against the creation of independent nation-states. They contend that such political organizations, while often being particularly violent in their creation, are inherently hierarchical, exclusionary, and Euro-centric, thus not representing a genuine emancipatory project.

Even before 2022, there was a noticeable trend toward *challenging prevailing ethnic and racial hierarchies* and fostering appreciation for minority and Indigenous cultures. Music, in particular, has come to symbolize broader language activism across Russia, echoing numerous local initiatives dedicated to the preservation and revival of minority cultures. For instance, musical groups such as Otyken,[196] which draws on aboriginal Siberian musical traditions, as well as Chuvash and Udmurt[197] indie artists that combine local folklore

---

[194] *Golod*, directed by Maksim Kurnikov, Aleksandr Arkhaneglskii, and Tatiana Sorokina (2022), www.youtube.com/watch?v=rXi3kBXMWo8; Amina Tsuntaeva, "Traditsionnyi mir i 'zhenskii vopros': Kavkaz v sovremennom kino," Daptar (July 5, 2023), https://daptar.ru/2023/07/05/tradicionnyj-mir-i-zhenskij-vopros-kavkaz-v-sovremennom-kino/; Dmitrii Volchek, "Tiur'ma narodov: Dekolonizatsiia postsovetskogo kinoekrana," Radio Svoboda, May 3, 2023, www.svoboda.org/a/tyurjma-narodov-dekolonizatsiya-postsovetskogo-kinoekrana/32388894.html; Mariia Chernykh, "Bol'shaia missiia malen'kogo kino," Doxa (February 7, 2022), https://doxajournal.ru/cinema_in_minority_languages.

[195] Madina Tlostanova, *What Does It Mean to Be Post-Soviet? Decolonial Art from the Ruins of the Soviet Empire* (Duke University Press, 2018).

[196] "Home," Otyken, https://otyken.ru.

[197] Radif Kashapov, "Elektropop, trep i dzhaz na iazykakh Povolzh'ia: Kratkii gid po aktual'noi muzyke iz Chuvashii i Udmurtii," Inde (February 19, 2019), https://inde.io/article/18541-elektropop-trep-i-dzhaz-na-yazykah-povolzhya-kratkiy-gid-po-aktualnoy-muzyke-iz-chuvashii-i-udmurtii.

and Russian and minority languages with modern music genres, have made their minority ethnic identity a point of pride.[198]

However, there is no clear definition of which groups should be recognized as Indigenous within the context of Russia. Traditionally, "Indigenous" has been associated with groups residing in the north and far east of the country, who often maintain traditional lifestyles. This raises the question of whether individuals from regions with significant population mixing, who may no longer speak their native languages, and/or who live in cities can still claim Indigenous status. Additionally, the history of Soviet deportations complicates terms like "settlers" and "colonists," particularly when applied to non-Russian ethnic groups who were forcibly relocated to Siberia and Central Asia.

Also issues of race have recently come to the forefront of public debate in Russia, particularly highlighted by the Russian-Tajik singer Manizha, who wittily described herself as *nedoslavianka* ("not quite a Slav"), while representing Russia in the Eurovision Song Contest 2021 with her song "Russian Woman." Her performance addressed women's rights violations, oppressive beauty standards, and ethnic and racial discrimination. Activists from Asiatic regions have been particularly vocal on these issues.[199] However, racial identification is complicated for non-Asiatic non-Russian ethnic groups. For instance, while the term Caucasian refers to "white" in the US context, in Russia Caucasians are referred to as "black" in racial discourse;[200] while Tatars and Udmurts, who might be "white-passing," are nevertheless frequently subject to exotification and discrimination (on the discussions of race in the scholarly field, see also Section 5).

Moreover, there are *de-secularizing projects*, where religion, particularly Islam, has emerged as a prism through which to reevaluate unequal power dynamics. Interlinked with other postcolonial regions in the Global South with significant Muslim populations while still infused with Soviet cultural symbolism, Russian-language Islamic discourse has developed a critique of Western imperialism – both in terms of its economic and cultural dimensions as well as the systems of dominance and subjugation that have been implemented by Russia toward its Muslim population, historically present or recently shaped by labor migration from Muslim-majority republics of Central Asia. Of

---

198 Egana Dzhabbarova, "Ot Manizhi do Tatarki: Kak rossiiskaia pop-muzyka uchitsia predstavliat' opyt Drugogo," Nozh (May 22, 2021), https://knife.media/decolonial-aesthesis/; Gulnaz Sibgatullina, "Changing the Tune: Can Russia's Ethnic Minority Musicians Challenge Imperialist Connotations of Russianess?," *Russia Post*, 2022, http://russiapost.net/regions/changing_the_tune.

199 E.g., Erzhen Erdeni, "Zapiski rossiiskoi aziatki: Pochemu nam stoit dekolonizirovat' krasotu?," Sygma, April 30, 2023, https://syg.ma/@f-center/zapiski-rossiiskoi-aziatki-pochiemu-nam-stoit-diekolonizirovat-krasotu-chast-1.

200 Bruce Baum, *The Rise and Fall of the Caucasian Race: A Political History of Racial Identity* (New York University Press, 2006), 219–33.

particular importance here are projects that are aimed at addressing the in-between position of migrant children growing up in Russia (such as the initiative "Children of Petersburg").

On the one hand, Islam-inspired discourses have offered alternative models of governance, community-building, and customary justice that draw inspiration from religious principles, thereby presenting alternatives to the Western-centric paradigms of liberal democracy and the nation-state.[201] On the other hand, they create tensions within the broader emancipatory movement in Russia, as the evolution of decolonial theory, which recognizes the intersectionality of oppression across gender, race, and ethnic identities,[202] has been cautious about endorsing initiatives that might potentially infringe on women's and LGBTQ+ rights.

Finally, decolonial activism remains a contested area, as there is always the risk of *reinforcing existing power hierarchies or reintroducing Western-centric ones*. Importing decolonial discourses from elsewhere and transplanting them into the post-socialist context has been referred to by Jan Sowa as "cargo modernization": "This model is based on the belief that the reproduction of Western ideological and economic standards will help bring us closer to modernity in the form in which it is imagined in the post-communist consciousness of the elites."[203] Decolonial activities in peripheral regions often become hijacked by power elites from the center (e.g., art exhibitions about northern cultures in Russia presented by curators from Moscow or Saint Petersburg without a critical assessment of their colonial approach).[204] This phenomenon reinforces the exoticization of minority cultures (e.g., documentaries on Muslim women in the Caucasus produced

---

[201] Robert Ware and Enver Kisriev, *Dagestan: Russian Hegemony and Islamic Resistance in the North Caucasus* (Routledge, 2014); Gulnaz Sibgatullina and Michael Kemper, "Between Salafism and Eurasianism: Geidar Dzhemal and the Global Islamic Revolution in Russia," in *Russia's Islam and Orthodoxy beyond the Institutions*, ed. Alfrid K. Bustanov and Michael Kemper (Routledge, 2019), 91–108; Danis Garaev, *Jihadism in the Russian-Speaking World: The Genealogy of a Post-Soviet Phenomenon* (Taylor & Francis, 2022); Egor Lazarev, *State-Building as Lawfare: Custom, Sharia, and State Law in Postwar Chechnya* (Cambridge University Press, 2023).

[202] Alexandra Biktimirova and Victoria Kravtsova, "Feminist Translocalities: Decolonial and Anti-Racist Feminisms in Russia and Beyond," *Baltic Worlds* (June 22, 2022), https://balticworlds .com/feminist-translocalities/.

[203] Anton Saifullaev, "Mezhdu imitatsiei i kritikoi: postkolonial'nye issledovaniia v Tsentral'noi Evrope (na primere Pol'shi)," *Novoe Literaturnoe Obozrenie* 6, no. 166 (2020), www.nlobooks .ru/magazines/novoe_literaturnoe_obozrenie/166_nlo_6_2020/article/22947/.

[204] Maria Huhmarniemi and Ekaterina Sharova, "Art from the Margins and Colonial Relations: To Listen or to Ban the Indigenous Voices from Russia?," in *Arctic Yearbook 2022: The Russian Arctic: Economics, Politics and Peoples*, ed. Lassi Heininen, Heather Exner-Pirot, and Justin Barnes (Arctic Yearbook, 2022), 3, https://arcticyearbook.com/arctic-yearbook/2022/2022-scholarly-papers/436-art-from-the-margins-and-colonial-relations-to-listen-to-or-to-ban-artists-voices-from-russia.

by the Russian liberal media)[205] as well as a general perception of such cultures that is centered around the promotion of exclusive ethnic nationalism or self-victimization.

Russia's position on the periphery of Europe (on the notion of "subaltern empire," see Section 5) further complicates defining its systems of oppression, especially when entering globalized debates: The emphasis on racial and ethnic minority groups in Russia may overshadow existing class issues. Minority ethnic groups in Russia, along with ethnic Russians from economically depressed regions, are still likely to be categorized within the "Global North," whereas much wealthier citizens of Gulf states are labeled as part of the "Global South" (though both terms are rightly contested in the academic and activist discourses, they remain popular in policymaking texts and popular debates). Furthermore, the label "ethnic Russian" obscures significant disparities between urban elites in cities like Moscow and Saint Petersburg and residents of economically distressed regions, whose economic conditions may be worse than those in relatively prosperous minority regions like Tatarstan.

## Conclusion

This section has presented a brief overview of the most recent Russian history. Specifically, we suggest three important takeaways.

First, contemporary Russia offers a fascinating case study of how situational claims related to (post-)colonial identity can be framed. A decade of decentralization, the 1990s, saw the blossoming of decolonial language, its capture by post-communist regional elites, and Russia's embrace of a neoliberal system; that is, the integration into neocolonial forms of oppression, where Russia's citizens can be regarded as both the oppressor and the oppressed.

Second, since the early 2000s, the Putin regime has gradually retaken control of both the policies and ideas related to colonialism. It has framed for itself a narrative of *right-wing decolonization* from what it views as an oppressive, postmodern and liberal neocolonialisn, which challenges Europe's traditional identity. At the same time, it has largely repressed grassroots decolonial initiatives, forcing them to survive in the interstices that the regime has left for civil society.

Finally, despite the tightening state control, grassroots decolonial movements in Russia have been in development. They are diverse in their ideological background and should not be automatically associated with Western-inspired liberalism, as some may come with another ideology, such as Islamism or

---

[205] Tsuntaeva, "Traditsionnyi mir."

communitarianism. The rise in activism following the full-scale invasion of Ukraine has largely been digital, relying on the connections fostered by online media platforms like Instagram, YouTube, and Telegram. As many activists had to flee the country in fear of prosecution, for them, digital activism remains the only available way to continue their work from abroad.

## 4 Decolonization and Its International Dimension

Far from being purely a bilateral issue between the colonized and their colonizers, decolonization never occurs in a vacuum. Instead, the process features both local decolonizing actors, who are looking for international recognition and support, and external actors, who have their own strategic interests in weakening a competitor and promoting new clients or partners. Countries of the so-called "Global South" often have an acute memory of previous decolonization struggles and continue to grapple with neocolonial or postcolonial hierarchies of power. In the Global North, meanwhile, decolonization was present in the political agenda of leftist movements throughout the twentieth century but has gained new potency in recent years as societal liberalization has challenged established racial and gender norms. Movements like Black Lives Matter have helped to renew public awareness about domestic decolonization as a culture war and a moral imperative that can be projected in foreign policy too.[206]

Both Russia and the United States have played a critical and contested role in this geopolitical struggle around the issue of decolonization throughout the twentieth century and into the twenty-first century. Indeed, both countries have built a large part of their mutual critique around the other's status as an empire, each claiming to occupy the moral high ground as the defender of the colonized. Meanwhile, local actors fighting for their own decolonization against one great power or another have long been underestimated, seen as simple pawns or puppets in a larger, geopolitical game. The current decolonization of knowledge requires recognizing this grassroots agency and its ability to shape realities on the ground.

It is therefore no surprise that the topic of decolonization has regained such visibility with the Russia–Ukraine War. After all, the war confirms that decolonization – understood not only as (re)gaining state sovereignty, but also as transforming other forms of power hierarchies – continues to be a major ideological signifier that helps societies to develop their strategic narrative and has become part of many countries' nation-building processes.

---

[206] Ty Solomon, "Up in the Air: Ritualized Atmospheres and the Global Black Lives Matter Movement," *European Journal of International Relations* 29, no. 3 (September 2023): 576–601; Giuliana Sorce and Delia Dumitrica, "Transnational Dimensions in Digital Activism and Protest," *Review of Communication* 22, no. 3: 157–74.

## Decolonization: A Longtime Battlefield for Competition between the USA and Russia

Decolonization crystallized as an object of geopolitical competition during the Cold War. The two superpowers victorious over Nazism, the United States and the Soviet Union, both denounced European colonialism and supported decolonization movements – even while engaging in para- or neocolonial practices in their own spheres of influence, the USA in Latin America and the Soviet Union in Central and Eastern Europe. Both backed some national liberation movements, sometimes providing them with military support. Korea, Vietnam, Afghanistan, Angola, El Salvador, Guatemala, and Nicaragua were the main theaters of these proxy wars.[207]

From its inception, Soviet internationalism supported anticolonial movements from within European colonies. In 1923, at the twelfth Congress of the Bolshevik Party, Nikolai Bukharin explained that "apart from the only consistent bearer of the communist uprising, the European and American proletariat, hundreds of millions of the colonial and semi-colonial slaves are taking part in the fight."[208] Paralleling proletarians in the developed and colonized nations in developing countries became a structural element of Soviet internationalist language.

In the post-World War II period, the Soviet Union imposed its strategic and political control over Central Europe, and while it, obviously, never framed it in a colonial language, many of the Soviet policies for the region had some colonial tones. The Warsaw Pact countries carried the brunt of colonial rule of the Soviet Union, such as "lack of sovereign power, restrictions on travel, military occupation, lack of convertible specie, a domestic economy ruled by the dominating state, and forced education in the colonizer's tongue."[209] These countries were integrated into the economic and scientific hierarchies within the Soviet Union, often through the relocation of Russian-speaking specialists. Notably, East Germany, Romania, and Czechoslovakia served as locations for intensive uranium mining, which had profound economic, environmental, and social (primarily health-related) consequences on local communities.

At the same time that the Soviet Union was dominating Central and Eastern Europe, on the international scene, Moscow was playing a crucial role in

---

[207] See, for instance, Natalia Telepneva, *Cold War Liberation: The Soviet Union and the Collapse of the Portuguese Empire in Africa, 1961–1975* (The University of North Carolina Press, 2022).

[208] Quoted in Maxim Khomyakov, "Russia: Colonial, Anticolonial, Postcolonial Empire?," *Social Science Information* 59, no. 2 (June 2020): 247.

[209] David Chioni Moore, "Is the Post- in Postcolonial the Post- in Post-Soviet? Toward a Global Postcolonial Critique," *PMLA* 116, no. 1: 111–28, here p. 121 as quoted in Sonja D. Schmid, "Nuclear Colonization? Soviet Technopolitics in the Second World," in *Entangled Geographies: Empire and Technopolitics in the Global Cold War*, ed. Gabrielle Hecht (MIT Press, 2011), 127.

supporting anti-imperial movements in developing countries, both in countries that were "fellow travelers" of socialism and in nonaligned countries. Soviet anti-racism campaigns were essential to the regime's conceptualization of its own political and moral identity. The decolonization of Asia and Africa provided new opportunities for Soviet diplomacy, and Central Asian republics, especially Uzbekistan, became a central ideological battlefront in the Cold War. No longer a threshold for exporting revolution, Central Asia was now presented as a model of socialist development for developing countries, an alternative path to modernization for countries emerging from colonialism.[210]

The Soviet regime gradually developed "rules of thumb" to follow in deciding whether and how to assist the varied anti-imperialist and separatist movements in the developing world.[211] One of the ways that Moscow sought to establish closer ties with African countries was through educational and training programs for African specialists. These programs aimed to educate Africans in various fields such as engineering, medicine, agriculture, economics, and political science, with the ultimate goal of fostering political alliances and economic cooperation between the Soviet Union and African nations.[212] Visible in Southeast Asia, Latin America, and to a lesser extent the Middle East, this strategy was epitomized by support for armed revolutionary movements in the three Portuguese colonies of Angola, Mozambique, and Guinea-Bissau, as well as for Mandela's ANC (African National Congress) in apartheid South Africa.[213]

Meanwhile, the USA and its allies presented themselves as the defenders of colonized nations under Soviet/Russian domination. This theme was not a new one: in the nineteenth century, democratic forces in Europe sided with the Polish independent movement and denounced the Tsarist Empire as a "prison of peoples," as the Marquis de Custine put it in his book *Russia in 1839*. The slogan was subsequently adopted by Vladimir Lenin himself in 1914 and then by Soviet revolutionary historiography to denounce the

---

[210] Artemy M. Kalinovsky, *Laboratory of Socialist Development: Cold War Politics and Decolonization in Soviet Tajikistan* (Cornell University Press, 2018); Hanna E. Jansen, "Peoples' Internationalism: Central Asian Modernisers, Soviet Oriental Studies and Cultural Revolution in the East (1936–1977)" (PhD diss., University of Amsterdam, 2020); James Mark and Paul Betts, eds, *Socialism Goes Global: The Soviet Union and Eastern Europe in the Age of Decolonisation* (Oxford University Press, 2022).

[211] Galia Golan, *The Soviet Union and National Liberation Movements in the Third World* (Routledge, 1988); Mark and Betts, *Socialism Goes Global*.

[212] E.g., Maxim Matusevich, "Journeys of Hope: African Diaspora and the Soviet Society," *African Diaspora* 1, no. 1–2 (2008): 53–85; Konstantinos Katsakioris, "Students from Portuguese Africa in the Soviet Union, 1960–74," *Journal of Contemporary History* 56, no. 1 (2021): 142–65.

[213] Telepneva, *Cold War Liberation*; Carol Saivetz, ed., *The Soviet Union in the Third World* (Routledge, 1989); Alvin Rubinstein, *Moscow's Third World Strategy* (Princeton University Press, 1989).

tsarist regime.[214] It later became one of the flagships of the American anti-communist struggle: the Anti-Bolshevik Bloc of Nations. The Bloc brought together many figures from among Russia's ethnic minorities such as Ukrainians, as well as White Russian émigrés who had collaborated with Nazi Germany during the war before being co-opted by the American and British intelligence services to lead the anti-Soviet struggle. Into the 1980s, several US institutions close to the CIA were working to promote "captive" Soviet nations and denounce communism as a new colonialism.[215]

As we can see from this brief overview, Russia/the Soviet Union and the United States have a long history of accusing the other of colonialism and instrumentalizing anticolonial fights to enhance their own influence. With the current Russia-Ukraine War and the decoupling of Russia from the West, decolonization has once again emerged as a central discursive theme of this longstanding geopolitical conflict.

## Russia's Branding as an Anticolonial Power

Beyond Soviet anti-imperialist internationalism, Russia can rely on a longer intellectual tradition – dating back to the nineteenth century – that sees the country as having been colonized by Europe. This vision, present already among the Slavophiles of the nineteenth century, was theorized by the founding fathers of Eurasianism in the 1920s. The Eurasianist movement aimed to put an end to the "cultural hegemony of the West"[216] by asserting the superiority of the East. It therefore subscribed to a Third Worldism *avant la lettre*, persuaded not only of non-Western cultures' right to differ, but also, and above all, of their ultimate superiority and Europe's decline.[217]

This feature of the self-coloniality debate reappeared in Russian intellectual life as soon as the Khrushchev Thaw allowed it. The theme of Russia's colonization by the West was actively advocated by the so-called Russian Party, the group of nationalists and conservative figures within the state and Communist Party apparatus.[218] For them, the Soviet experiment – having been inspired by a Western European ideology, Marxism – should be read as

---

[214] Astolphe de Custine, La Russie en 1839, Third Edition (Amyot, 1846), 470–71, https://fr.wikisource.org/wiki/La_Russie_en_1839; Vladimir Lenin, "K voprosu o Natsional'noi politike," 1914, http://libelli.ru/works/25-5.htm

[215] Kyle Burke, *Revolutionaries for the Right: Anticommunist Internationalism and Paramilitary Warfare in the Cold War* (The University of North Carolina Press, 2018); Benjamin Tromly, *Cold War Exiles and the CIA: Plotting to Free Russia* (Oxford University Press, 2019).

[216] Georgii Vernadskii, "Mongol'skoe igo v russkoi istorii," *Evraziiskaia khronika* V (1927): 155.

[217] On Eurasianist anticolonialism, see Sergei Glebov, "Whither Eurasia? History of Ideas in an Imperial Situation," *Ab Imperio*, no. 2 (2008): 345–76.

[218] Yitzhak M. Brudny, *Reinventing Russia: Russian Nationalism and the Soviet State, 1953–1991* (Harvard University Press, 2000).

a Western colonization of Russia. Similarly, the abrupt "shock therapy" of the 1990s was taken by all the conservative and nationalist forces as a new form of Western colonization; liberalism was interpreted as a neocolonial imposition. Over time, Vladimir Putin's speeches have come to deploy an anticolonial tone in describing Russia's relationship to the West: He has condemned Western normative domination (the theme of sovereignty), Western economic domination (the theme of the theft of natural resources by foreign companies), and Western cultural domination (the theme of anti-LGBT+ rights).

The revival of this Russian discourse about the colonial West has targeted not only a domestic audience, but also international ones. While the Soviet legacy of fighting against US imperialism largely collapsed with the end of the Soviet Union, the revival of tensions between the USA and Russia in the 2010s contributed to reactivating that tradition and its international networks.

With its full-scale invasion of Ukraine, the Russian leadership has reactivated the Soviet anticolonial repertoire – presenting itself as an anticolonial force partnering with countries of the Global South to oppose Western hegemony. In 2019, Putin made his first mentions of the Western "colonial mindset" toward formerly colonized countries and the West's attempts to prevent Russia from building partnerships with African nations.[219] The 2023 Foreign Policy Concept of the Russian Federation also explicitly deployed the notion of colonialism in its characterization of the West.[220]

## European Memory Wars and Russia's Imperial/Colonial Past

Meanwhile, a narrative of fighting against Russian imperialism has reemerged in the West. It has been closely associated with the memory wars raging in Central and Eastern Europe regarding their twentieth-century past.

Led by the Baltic states and Poland, now joined by Georgia, Ukraine, and Moldova, a large scholarly and political movement reassessing the history of post-World War II Europe has taken shape. It began in the mid 2000s, when the Central European countries joined the European Union and NATO and challenged the Western view of the postwar period as an era of stability and prosperity as one that excludes the lived realities of the countries of the former socialist bloc, for whom the postwar period is synonymous with the loss of their strategic autonomy (and, in the case of the Baltic states, their sovereignty) and

---

[219] Vladimir Putin, "Interv'iu informatsionnomu agenstvu TASS," Kremlin.ru, October 21, 2019, www.kremlin.ru/events/president/news/61858.

[220] Ministry of Foreign Affairs of the Russian Federation, "The Concept of the Foreign Policy of the Russian Federation," March 31, 2023, https://mid.ru/en/foreign_policy/fundamental_docu ments/1860586/.

being cut off from their European identity.[221] Closely linked to this reassessment has been the reinterpretation of the Soviet Union's role in the war – as Moscow initially collaborated with Nazi Germany between 1939 and 1941 before becoming its enemy – and of the 1945 victory as being not only the triumph of the Allied forces, but also the abandonment of Central and Eastern Europe to the Soviets. As then Lithuanian President Valdas Adamkus stated bluntly, for the Baltic states, May 9, 1945, was the day "we traded Hitler for Stalin."[222]

These memory wars, which have provoked a fierce reaction on the Russian side – including a proactive memory policy[223] – have built on the idea of decolonizing from Russia-centric narratives of the past century. They connect decommunization measures such as lustration and transitional justice (the establishment of policies of restitution and compensation, the creation of truth commissions, and the opening of archives) with cultural and strategic de-Russification measures such as demoting Russian in favor of the national language, rewriting history textbooks to present the Soviet past negatively and as a continuation of the tsarist regime, changing the names of cities and streets, and removing Soviet-era monuments.

For both governments and activists in Central and Eastern Europe, reading the postwar Soviet domination as colonial allows them to position their own cultural struggles in parallel with intra-European and Global South struggles. The call for rescue from a post-socialist or post-Soviet "ghetto" that would continue to insist on their former belonging to the Eastern bloc has been a driving force behind these new cultural and memory policies.

The denouncing of Russia's imperialism also become a central part of Central and Eastern European nation-building. Constructing a parallel with the Shoah, their new historiographies have built for themselves what Wilfried Jilge calls "national Holocausts" – victim status and the perceived moral high ground that goes along with it.[224] They have developed a strategy of "memory appropriation" in order to make their national suffering under communism the cornerstone of their new, post-communist sense of identity and belonging to Europe.[225] These new historiographies and memories simultaneously achieve several goals: They cultivate renewed pride in the country's own history and uniqueness; avoid direct discussions of

---

[221] Nikolai Koposov, *Memory Laws, Memory Wars: The Politics of the Past in Europe and Russia* (Cambridge University Press, 2017).

[222] Richard Holbrooke, "The End of the Romance," *The Washington Post*, February 16, 2005, www.washingtonpost.com/wp-dyn/articles/A27622–2005Feb15.html.

[223] Jade McGlynn, *Memory Makers: The Politics of the Past in Putin's Russia* (Bloomsbury Academic, 2023).

[224] Wilfried Jilge, "Zmahannia zhertv," *Kritika* 5 (2006): 14–17.

[225] Jelena Subotić, *Yellow Star, Red Star: Holocaust Remembrance after Communism* (Cornell University Press, 2019).

collaborationist groups that took part in the Holocaust and mass killings of civilians;[226] and facilitate an easy sense of Europeanness by situating the main other – Russia – as a non-European power.[227]

Other countries have engaged in these decolonial practices to a lesser extent. In Central Asia and the Caucasus, with the exception of Georgia until recently, the authorities have remained hesitant to cut ties with Moscow and have therefore toned down any anticolonial narratives perceived as too radical. They have, however, authorized some forms of de-Russification of the public sphere, including limiting the use of Russian in favor of the national language, nationalizing public memory, limiting Russian media's outreach, and de-Russifying national holidays and toponyms. In the early 1990s, anticolonial narratives were expressed in Central Asia, for instance, by small intellectual circles with a pan-Turkic or Islamist sensibility; but these were rapidly marginalized and/or repressed by the region's regimes.

Three decades later, a new generation of anticolonial activists has emerged; they are able to reach a broader audience via social media and are being given more space by the authorities. In Kazakhstan and Kyrgyzstan, anticolonial narratives gained some visibility when both countries joined the Eurasian Economic Union in 2015 and during the centenary of the 1916 Steppe Revolt a year later – on both occasions, their proponents denounced Russian imperialism old and new, as well as their own authorities' ambivalence toward it.[228] With the full-scale invasion of Ukraine, these anticolonial stances have gained more visibility among some constituencies in Central Asia.

## The New Activism of "Dismantling Russia"

The idea that Russia is still an empire and needs to follow the Soviet Union's fate was present in the West in the early 1990s, when the new Russia was still a largely decentralized country where a weak center was fighting with independentist (in the case of Chechnya) and sovereigntist (in the case of Tatarstan) claims. This narrative largely disappeared in the mid 1990s, advocated only by small groups connected to Chechens in exile or to older diasporas such as the Circassians, who have regularly tried to bring the

---

[226] Stefan Rohdewald, "Post-Soviet Remembrance of the Holocaust and National Memories of the Second World War," *Forum for Modern Language Studies* 44, no. 2 (April 2008): 173–84.

[227] Maria Mälksoo, "Nesting Orientalisms at War: World War II and the 'Memory War' in Eastern Europe," in *Orientalism and War,* ed. Tarak Barkawi and Ketih Stanski (Oxford University Press, 2013), 176–95. For a general overview by a Russian historian, see Gennadii Bordiugov, "*Voina pamiati" na postsovetskom prostranstve* (AIRO-XXI, 2011).

[228] See Marlene Laruelle, "Which Future for National-Patriots? The Landscape of Kazakh Nationalism," in *Kazakhstan in the Making*, ed. Marlene Laruelle (Lexington, 2016), 155–80.

attention of the Western community to what they define as the Circassian genocide perpetrated by Tsarist Russia.[229]

The violence of Russia's full-scale invasion of Ukraine in 2022, as well as the imperial tone of Moscow's justifications for invasion, immediately reactivated the theme of dismantling Russia. In the US media and policy world, narratives about dismembering Russia have proliferated. The anti-kleptocracy journalist Casey Michel has advocated, for instance, that the West "complete the project that began in 1991. It must seek to fully decolonize Russia."[230] Several think tanks and institutions with a clear pro-NATO and Russia-skeptical orientation, such as the Jamestown Foundation, the Hudson Institute, the Center for European Policy Analysis (CEPA), and the Helsinki Commission, have published articles and op-eds or organized events calling for or supporting the collapse of the Russian Federation.[231]

The majority of this new activism is led by Russian citizens now in exile. The section of the Russian opposition abroad, long insensitive to the issue of ethnic diversity, has had to take more explicit positions. It has realized that the theme of decolonizing Russia – in the sense of dismantling it – has resonance in the West and can be paired judiciously with criticisms of the authoritarian drift of the Putin regime. Both the Free Russia Forum, created in 2016 and led by Garry Kasparov and Ivan Tyutrin, and the Congress of People's Deputies, which presents itself as a transitional government for Russia – with figures such as Ilia Ponomarev, a former Russian MP who was the only one to vote against Crimea's annexation in 2014, and Andrei Illarionov, a former advisor to Putin who has also worked for the libertarian Cato Institute think tank in Washington, DC – now use the notions of empire and imperialism to describe Russia, often conflating these with "authoritarian" and "Putin's regime."

With the war, there have also appeared more radical organizations that have the sole aim of dismantling the Russian Federation. The most extreme of these, the Forum of the Free Nations of Post-Russia, was launched in Prague in July 2022, publishing its manifesto in Gdansk in September of that year and

---

[229] "Circassian" is the term used to describe the Indigenous people of the Western North Caucasus, also known as Adygue, who were deported and killed en masse during and after the Russo-Circassian War (1763–1864) and Russia's conquest of the Caucasus.

[230] Casey Michel, "Decolonize Russia," *The Atlantic*, May 27, 2022, www.theatlantic.com/ideas/archive/2022/05/russia-putin-colonization-ukraine-chechnya/639428/.

[231] Janusz Bugajski, *Failed State: A Guide to Russia's Rupture* (Lynne Rienner Publishers, 2022); "Decolonizing Russia: A Moral and Strategic Imperative," Helsinki Commission, June 23, 2022, www.csce.gov/international-impact/events/decolonizing-russia; "A New Architecture for Northern Eurasia: The Sixth Free Nations of Post-Russia Forum," April 25–26, 2023, www.youtube.com/watch?v=x45dAvJuYH0; Edward Lucas, "What Will Russia Look Like after Putin?," Center For European Policy Analysis (CEPA), March 5, 2023, https://cepa.org/article/russias-collapse-ringside-seat/.

some "Brussels Protocols" in January 2023 during a visit to the European Parliament. In its two years of existence, it has organized over a dozen congresses, including one in Washington, DC, and one in Tokyo. The movement brings together about forty groups/associations representing the forty-one supposed new "states" that will allegedly succeed Russia. The Forum's map of the forty-one new states features some improbable entities: For instance, Moscow would become part of the Zales'e Federation, with its capital in the small provincial city of Vladimir, meaning Moscow would no longer be the capital of anything; South Sakhalin and the Kurils would be given to Japan; Chechnya would absorb about half of Dagestan; and the proposed Nogai republic, with its capital supposedly in Astrakhan, would not actually include any ethnically Nogai territories.

A second organization, the Free Nations League, espouses similar goals, such as "consolidating anti-imperialist forces, preparing cadres for statehood, looking for allies on the international scene, obtaining real sovereignty for the subjects of the Russian Federation, and realizing the right to self-determination."[232] It brings together mostly Kalmyk, Bahskir, Erzyan (Erzyans speak a Mordvinic, Finno-Uralic language), and Buryat activists and has "observers" from Sakha, Ingushetia, and among the Indigenous peoples of the Arctic. Its impact likewise seems quite modest, as it enjoys fewer than 3,000 subscribers on Telegram and 700 followers on Facebook.

The relationship between these two institutions and the more established liberal opposition is ambivalent. The Free Russia Forum does not comment on the debate about dismantling Russia and seems to avoid taking a position, while the Congress of People's Deputies is closer to the separatists. It declares, for instance, that the future of the Russian Federation should be decided by the free choice of its peoples based on the right to self-determination.[233] It also recognizes the Chechen government of Ichkeria (the name of the near-independent state structure of Chechnya in the 1990s), and one of its key members, Ilya Pomonarev, is also a central figure of the Post-Russia Forum.

Another group of actors in the decolonial fight are Russians fighting in the war on the Ukrainian side as part of the Ukrainian Foreign Legion. Having passed background checks conducted by the Main Directorate of Intelligence of the Ukrainian Ministry of Defense, they enjoy access to different forms of support, from simple logistical assistance to the provision of weapons and integration into the Ukrainian armed forces. All the foreign legions made up

---

[232] Free Nations League, "Sobytiia v zhizni Ligi Svobodnykh Natsii," July 30, 2023, https://freenationsleague.org/ru/home.html.

[233] Ilya Ponomarev, "Osnovopolagaiushchaia Deklaratsiia S"ezd Narodnykh Deputatov," Congress of People's Deputies, November 4, 2022, https://rosdep.online/declaration_snd/.

of post-Soviet citizens claim to fight against Russian imperialism and call for the dismantling of the Russian Federation.

The most radical units are the Russian Volunteers Corps (RDK), made up of neo-Nazis, and the Legion "Freedom of Russia" (LSR), initially formed by Russian prisoners of war in Ukraine and then enlarged by the addition of Russian volunteers. Both advocate for the dissolution of the Federation. Also present in Ukraine are several Muslim battalions, chiefly the two Chechen ones – named after Sheikh Mansur and Dzhokhar Dudaev – that have been fighting against Russia and the Kadyrov regime for years, as well as several newer ones: Krym for Crimean Tatars, Turan for Turkic-speaking nations, a Siberian battalion for the Asiatic peoples of Russian Siberia and the Far East, and a Georgian battalion that parallels Georgia's anticolonial fight with Ukraine's.[234] It remains difficult to verify these battalions' statistical reality, probably numbering a few hundred members.

Ukraine, too, has obviously become a central actor in the fight for dismantling Russia. As early as 2019, Kyiv supported the self-proclaimed Erzyan government.[235] In fall 2022, Kyiv issued a general declaration of support for the self-determination of minorities within the Russian Federation[236] and recognized the Chechen Republic of Ichkeria as "temporarily occupied" by Russia.[237] In summer 2023, the Ukrainian Parliament, the Verkhovna Rada, launched a special commission to elaborate a state policy for "Russia's unfree nations."[238]

Poland is involved too. Former Polish president Lech Walesa invited the West to organize the revolt of the "60 peoples who got colonized by Russia," without which Russia would be reduced of a country of 140 million to about 50 million people.[239] The idea of reducing Russia to the medieval Moscow principality goes hand in hand with the competing geopolitical dream of creating "Intermarium": a new regional entity stretching from the Baltic Sea to the Black Sea that would be made up of countries united in their desire to protect

---

234 Jean-Francois Ratelle, Mira Seales, and Agnes Wenger, "Foreign Fighters in Ukraine: Multiple Ideological Agendas, One Tactical Goal," PONARS Eurasia Policy memo, no. 852, August 2023.

235 Ramazan Alpaut, "Ukrainets Boliaen' Syres' ofitsial'no vozglavil erziianskoe natsional'noe dvizhenie," Idel.Realii, September 13, 2019, www.idelreal.org/a/30162398.html.

236 Free Nations League, "Ukraina povyshaet stavki: Verkhovnaia Rada ofitsial'no zaiavila o prave poraboshchennykh moskvoi narodov na samoopredelenie," October 6, 2022, https://bit.ly/415m1TT.

237 "Verkhovnaia rada Ukrainy priznala nezavisimost' Ichkerii," *Kommersant'*, October 18, 2022, www.kommersant.ru/doc/5620347.

238 Anti-Imperial Bloc of Peoples (ABN), "V Verkhovnoi Rade Ukrainy initsiiruiut sozdanie vremennoi spetsial'noi komissii po razrabotke gosudarstvennoi politiki otnositel'no poraboshchennykh narodov," July 28, 2023, https://bit.ly/3ErkDCj.

239 Darius Rochebin, "Interview – Lech Walesa: 'Il ne faut pas seulement libérer l'Ukraine mais la Russie'," TFI Info, July 8, 2022, https://bit.ly/416GM1m.

Europe from Russian imperialism.[240] Anna Fotyga, a current Polish MEP and former Minister of Foreign Affairs, holds a leading role in the Free Nations League. Supporters of these separatist movements can also be found in Japan, for instance among the MPs who organized the August 2023 Forum of Free Nations meeting.

## Performing Symbolic Politics

Like many activist lobbies, the movements calling for the dismantling of Russia are only dubiously representative and do not comprise a credible political alternative. Instead, their actions should be read mostly as performative – as a gesture of symbolic politics at a time when the war has reactivated Russia's international visibility, even if in a negative way. This performance targets Western decision-makers and funders more than it does Russia's ethnically diverse population, even if in some cases activists may enjoy respect in their own communities in Russia.

The Russian so-called liberal opposition is itself divided between those who believe a democratic regime would be enough to ensure the rights of ethnic minorities, those who defend a larger decentralization, and those who wish for the country's collapse. As they live mostly abroad, the secessionists have limited connections on the ground and a modest reach on social media (their audiences are minimal compared with those of Russian liberal media now abroad, such as *Meduza* or *Dozhd'*, which have more than a million followers on Telegram). They can foster hype and draw attention, but they have so far failed to delineate credible paths toward Russia's transformation. Even if the population they represent were to support a secessionist agenda – and we have no data that would support or challenge this hypothesis – they have not offered any proposals on how they would organize the transfer of power, the creation of new institutions, the dismantling of security services, the management of the military structures and potentially nuclear arsenals on their soil, the risk of border tensions with their new neighbors, the development of economic and political programs, the place of ethnic Russians and the Russian language in their constitution, etc. All these programmatic aspects lack detailed attention to date.

The geopolitical instrumentalization of the topic of Russia's decolonization has not become the core of Europe's or the USA's foreign policy toward Russia but several important institutions such as the Organization for Security and Co-operation in Europe (OSCE) or the European parliament, as well as some EU countries such as Poland, regularly assert that peace can be achieved by the

---

[240] Marlene Laruelle and Ellen Rivera, "Imagined Geographies of Central and Eastern Europe: The Concept of Intermarium," *IERES Occasional Papers* (March 2019), www.ifri.org/sites/default/files/atoms/files/laruelle-rivera-ieres_papers_march_2019_1.pdf.

decolonization of the Russian Federation. One can imagine that the risks of civil war and nuclear proliferation associated with such a dismantling may cool decisionmakers' heads.

All the movements that promote the dismantling of Russia employ very reified definitions of identity. Even those that present themselves as analytical platforms for experts in exile fail to discuss how ethnicity is operationalized. The forty-one "nations" of the Post-Russia Forum treat as equal both the deeply ingrained sociological realities of ethnic minorities and pseudo-regional identities with no reality on the ground – rendering a disservice to genuine grassroots grievances.

## Conclusion

As we have discussed here, the international aspect of the "decolonizing Russia" debate is nothing new. First of all, classic decolonization by definition has foreign policy implications, as it implies changes to state borders. But even when decolonization is not about state sovereignty, but rather about challenging great powers' spheres of influence and their toolkits of "hard" and "soft" power, decolonization implies an interaction between domestic and foreign policies, between local and external actors.

With the full-scale invasion of Ukraine, Russia is now presented as the "sick man" of Europe, as a weakened Ottoman Empire was described in the late nineteenth century. The parallel is perhaps striking, but caveats apply: While presenting a country as imperial or colonial may reflect its genuine features, it may also be part of a strategy of de-legitimation and "othering." It is a label that implies political superiority and connects a moral aspect with a geopolitical objective. As Nathalie Koch explains, there are "moral geographies of the liberal and illiberal, the democratic and autocratic, the good and bad, which are inextricable from the actual conduct of geopolitics. . . . [By presenting the West] as inherently morally superior, these narratives advance an Orientalist worldview, whereby authoritarian political configurations are portrayed as essentially foreign and 'backward.'"[241]

It is therefore important to keep in mind the context in which the international debate on "decolonizing Russia" is taking place. US society and, to a lesser degree, its European counterparts are preoccupied with identitarian trends and are becoming polarized by culture-war discourses that have become global. These are easily translatable into a decolonizing language that speaks to the progressivist or liberal constituencies for whom Russia embodies many different negative features: the traditional masculinity and bravado of its leader, the

---

[241] Natalie Koch, "Post-Triumphalist Geopolitics: Liberal Selves, Authoritarian Others," *ACME: An International Journal for Critical Geographies* 18, no. 4 (2019): 912.

anti-LGBT attitudes of its society, imperialism toward its own minorities and neighbors, aggression and norm violations on the international scene.

In Russia's neighbors such as Central Asian countries, new generations of decolonial activists consider that lifting Russian cultural dominance is even more important than gaining political independence, either because they already have the latter or because they do not have elaborated programs and popular support for it. Framing the fight against the Russian regime as a decolonial struggle helps these activists to find a common language with liberal segments of Western societies and feel less marginalized from global cultural fights. It also facilitates the operationalization of lobbying strategies and policies that combine domestic forces with international partnerships.

## 5 Decolonization as Scholarship

Russia's full-scale invasion of Ukraine on February 24, 2022 sent shockwaves through academic circles. One significant response to the war's atrocities has been a growing call for the decolonization of research methodologies, dominant analytical frameworks, and curricula related to the study of Eastern Europe, Eurasia, Central Asia, and Russia. In the months following the invasion, there has been a notable increase in the number of conferences, workshops, and summer schools centered around the theme of decolonization. The aim of these has been to draw the focus away from Moscow-centrism and instead emphasize the perspectives of other nations of the region, first and foremost Ukrainian perspectives, as well as those of non-Russian minorities within Russia. Now, a whole movement has been launched to bring attention – in the form of new projects, funding opportunities, and scholarships – to regions that have historically lived in the "shadow" of Russian influence.

However, as the decolonization movement gains momentum within academia, numerous scholars have started to voice their concerns. The debate surrounding the application of postcolonial theories to Russian and Soviet contexts has been ongoing since at least the early 2000s, with a substantial body of existing scholarship often being overlooked amid the current discourse. Furthermore, postcolonial theory itself has fallen foul of various shortcomings and limitations, particularly when applied to the heterogeneous contexts of countries that underwent political and economic transitions after 1989–91 – a critical aspect that still demands careful consideration and discussion, as neoliberal transition in many ways has helped to perpetuate some forms of normative dominance from the West. This section aims to provide an overview of the postcolonialism debate in academia with relation to Russia, highlighting key areas of tension and suggesting potential avenues for future research.

## Russian's (Self-)Orientalism

While not exclusively confined to the labels of (de)colonial or postcolonial studies, historians have consistently employed critical perspectives to scrutinize the dynamics of unequal power, systems of oppression, and subjugation within the domain of Russian imperial history. The essence of this scholarship revolves around an analysis of the strategies employed by the Russian Empire to govern and assimilate various Indigenous populations into its imperial framework.

Scholarship also has sought to uncover instances where the Russian imperial project exhibited similarities to, or directly borrowed elements from, Western colonial empires, such as in the governance of the Kazakh steppes and Turkestan.[242] At the same time, research has also explored the unique attributes that distinguish the Russian imperial experience. These traits are often linked to Russia's exceptional geographical characteristics as a continental empire, rather than an overseas one; the wide array of communities it sought to govern; and the impact of cultural elements, with the Russian Orthodox Church playing a key role in shaping certain institutions and policies.

One particularly fruitful area of analysis involves the exploration of Russian Orientalism, drawing upon the analytical framework developed by Edward Said in *Orientalism* (1978).[243] On the one hand, the Russian Empire cultivated a robust school of Oriental studies that, much like Western Orientalism, focused on classifying and describing the peoples of its "inner Orient." On the other hand, as shown by Viatcheslav Morozov, the country elites identified Russia as a subaltern empire that colonized itself "on behalf of the global capitalist core while itself being integrated into European international society."[244] Thus, according to Morozov, as part of a highly complex relationship, Russia both resented and sought to emulate the West.[245]

---

[242] Just to give a few examples: Alexander Morrison, *The Russian Conquest of Central Asia: A Study in Imperial Expansion, 1814–1914* (Cambridge University Press, 2020); Paolo Sartori and Pavel Shabley, *Eksperimenty imperii: adat, shariat i proizvodstvo znanii v Kazakkhskoi stepi* (NLO, 2019).

[243] Edward W. Said, *Orientalism* (Pantheon Books, 1978); David Schimmelpenninck van der Oye, "The Curious Fate of Edward Said in Russia," *Études de Lettres* 296, no. 2–3 (2014): 81–94; Vladimir Bobrovnikov, "Orientalizm – ne dogma, a rukovodstvo k deistviiu? O perevodakh i ponimanii knigi E.V. Saida v Rossii," in *Orientalizm vs orientalistika*, ed. Vladimir Bobrovnikov ("Sadra," 2016), 53–77; Svetlana Gorshenina, "Orientalism, Postcolonial and Decolonial Frames on Central Asia: Theoretical Relevance and Applicability," in *European Handbook of Central Asian Studies*, ed. Bruno De Cordier, Adrien Fauve, and Jeroen Van Den Bosch (Ibidem-Verlag, 2021), 177–243.

[244] Viatcheslav Morozov, *Russia's Postcolonial Identity: A Subaltern Empire in a Eurocentric World* (Palgrave Macmillan, 2015), 32.

[245] Tamar Koplatadze, "Theorising Russian Postcolonial Studies," *Postcolonial Studies* 22, no. 4 (2019): 476.

The idea of Russia engaging in a unique form of self-colonization was first articulated by Alexander Etkind in *Internal Colonization: Russia's Imperial Experience*. The concept of "internal colonization" posits that Russia not only welcomed foreigners to take on the role of conquerors but also encouraged its own elite to adopt a stance resembling that of the British or French in their overseas colonies. According to Etkind, this self-colonization involved a discursive transformation of the Russian peasantry into the Other, marked by distinct identifiers of alterity, including the wearing of a full beard, religious affiliation, and the assignment of estate status.[246]

This argument has attracted much attention, as well as critique, particularly for blurring the experiences of non-Russian peoples subjected to more "classical" forms of colonization at the hand of the Russian state with the experiences of the Russian peasantry.[247] One way to view these two dimensions of colonial violence, affecting both the Russian peasantry and ethnic minorities, is as not mutually exclusive but rather creating space for both victims and perpetrators of external and internal colonialism. This perspective underscores the intricate and interconnected nature of Russia's colonial history, where external and internal dynamics often converged and coexisted.[248]

## The Notion of Eurasia: Global History and Imperiality

Beyond employing postcolonial theory to examine the Russo-Soviet peripheries, scholars have also studied how the Soviet experience shaped postcolonial theory, such as scholar Rossen Djagalov, who explored how the Soviet experience shaped postcolonial theory through its associated literary and cinematic output. One of the key arguments advanced by this genealogy is the significant challenge it poses to the notion that postcolonial studies has been exclusively a Western creation, a claim that has occasionally been voiced by critics from the Global South.[249]

Indeed, since the 1990s there has been a concerted effort to move beyond the oversimplified Europe–Asia binary in analyzing the Russian case. The revival of the notion of "Eurasia" in academia, while widely criticized now for potentially bolstering Russia's hegemonic project, has provided fertile soil for reconnecting the field of Soviet studies with broader world history. Scholarship on global history and on the history of globalization, which aim to challenge

---

[246] Alexander Etkind, *Internal Colonization: Russia's Imperial Experience* (Polity Press, 2011).

[247] E.g., Alexander S. Morrison, "Review of Alexander Etkind 'Internal Colonization. Russia's Imperial Experience'," *Ab Imperio*, no. 3 (2013): 445–57.

[248] Alexander Etkind, Dirk Uffelmann, and Ilya Kukulin, eds, *Tam, vnutri: Praktiki vnutrennei kolonizatsii v kulturnoi istorii Rossii* (NLO, 2012), 24; Uffelmann, "Postcolonial Theory," 138.

[249] Rossen Djagalov, *From Internationalism to Postcolonialism: Literature and Cinema between the Second and the Third Worlds* (McGill-Queen's University Press, 2020); Robert J. C. Young, "The Soviet Invention of Postcolonial Studies," *boundary 2* 50, no. 2 (2023): 133–56.

Western-centric assumptions, has facilitated state-of-the-art research on trans-regional, continental, worldwide history – of commodities for instance – in which Eurasia has been an important component (often connected with the revival of the notion of the Silk Roads).[250]

As Mark von Hagen discussed in a landmark article of 2004,[251] the term "Eurasia," though ill-defined, symbolizes the end of the discipline of Soviet studies and the reintegration of the region into current social science trends, thereby creating a new paradigm in which rich discussions can be had regarding notions such as empire and nation-state, borders and boundaries, diasporas, Russia's self-colonization and Orientalization, etc. As he explained, "the Eurasia anti-paradigm does not pretend to be a hegemonic new paradigm that excludes the development of other approaches or questions," but indicates "an opening up of the horizon of historical scholarship to new framings, topics, and dynamics and to 'return' the Eurasian space to world history."[252] Such a focus also enables critical analysis of anti-modernist politics, which runs deep in Russian intellectual thought and allows us to capture "how a properly postcolonial theory can espouse deeply conservative scenarios of emancipation (sometimes quite fascist in their outlook), and have a hidden restorationist agenda and imperialist potential of its own."[253]

This observation regarding Russia's ambivalent place in the field of colonial studies led scholars associated with the *Ab Imperio* journal to suggest that "a colonial situation can be identified as an acute epistemological problem regardless of the actual colonial experience."[254] Since the mid 2000s, *Ab Imperio* has taken the leading role in addressing the imperial/colonial debate regarding the study of Russia and Eurasia, arguing in favor of a perspective where empire is seen as "a mode of addressing the fundamental imperial situation." In contrast to Georges Balandier's concept of a colonial situation characterized by stable relationships of dominance and subordination within a closed system, the editors of *Ab Imperio* argue that the Russian imperial experience is shaped by diversity and change within an open system. It involves the coexistence and overlap of various classifications of diversity, each with its own principles of hierarchy, without a single, universal "exchange rate" between them.[255]

---

[250] See, for instance, Peter Frankopan, *The Silk Roads: A New History of the World* (Vintage, 2017).

[251] Mark von Hagen, "Empires, Borderlands, and Diasporas: Eurasia as Anti-Paradigm for the Post-Soviet Era," *American Historical Review* 109, no. 2 (2004): 445–68.

[252] Ibid., 467–68; Koplatadze, "Theorising Russian Postcolonial Studies," 473.

[253] Ilya Gerasimov, Sergey Glebov, and Marina Mogilner, "The Postimperial Meets the Postcolonial: Russian Historical Experience and the Postcolonial Moment," *Ab Imperio*, no. 2 (2013): 97–135, here p. 108.

[254] Ibid., 102.

[255] Ilya Gerasimov, "The Russian Imperial Situation: Before and after the Nation-State," *Ab Imperio*, no. 4 (2022): 31–59, here p. 43.

In this new imperial history as advocated by *Ab Imperio*, individuals and groups are perceived as occupying multiple social roles and operating at various levels of societal organization. Through the imperial lens, we can explore how and when individuals "switch" between different roles and strategies, altering the meaning and mode of their actions and even their identities: "The oppressed anti-imperial rebels can act as colonizers, and the imperial administration can perform as nation-builders for minority groups."[256] Indeed, an examination of Indigenous communities unveils intricate hierarchies and solidarities.[257] Muslims of the Volga-Ural region, being one of the most sizeable non-Russian populations of the Empire and among the first to be conquered, were early adopters of the imperial framework for governing minority groups. At the same time, Kazan Tatars capitalized on Russia's commercial and military expansion into Central Asia and positioned themselves as leaders capable of introducing Islamic modernity to the broader Muslim population of Russia, effectively becoming themselves agents of colonial expansion in the process.[258]

## Debating the Coloniality of the Soviet Experience

Scholarly analysis of the Soviet system as an iteration of colonialism is closely linked to the political aspirations of the nation-states that emerged after the fall of the Soviet Union. These newly independent states, to varying degrees and through various discursive frameworks, have consistently asserted their right to adopt a postcolonial stance. In doing so, they seek to assert their "sovereign subjectivity of the formerly oppressed."[259]

This perspective highlights the importance of distinguishing between diverse experiences within the framework of postcolonial analysis. On one side, one can find Central Asia, Transcaucasia, and regions inside Russia, whose languages, religions, and social and cultural histories differ from those of Russia, and hence were subjected to a more intense Russification and more invasive forms of acculturation (colonial par excellence). Much recent scholarship, particularly on Central Asia, has productively critiqued prevailing understandings of the Soviet experience.[260] On the other side, Ukraine and Belarus, though forcefully

---

[256] Gerasimov et al., "The Postimperial Meets the Postcolonial," 131.

[257] Paul Werth, *The Tsar's Foreign Faiths: Toleration and the Fate of Religious Freedom in Imperial Russia* (Oxford University Press, 2014); Robert C. Geraci, *Window on the East: National and Imperial Identities in Late Tsarist Russia* (Cornell University Press, 2001).

[258] Ross, *Tatar Empire.*     [259] Gerasimov et al., "The Postimperial Meets the Postcolonial," 122.

[260] See, for instance, Erica Marat, "Introduction: 30 Years of Central Asian Studies – the Best Is Yet to Come," *Central Asian Survey* 40, no. 4 (2021): 477–82, https://doi.org/10.1080/02634937.2021.1994921; Botakoz Kassymbekova and Aminat Chokobaeva, "On Writing Soviet History of Central Asia: Frameworks, Challenges, Prospects," *Central Asian Survey* 40, no. 4 (2021): 483–503, DOI: 10.1080/02634937.2021.1976728.

incorporated into the tsarist and then Soviet systems, with all their destructive population and territorial management, could still enjoy some of the privileges associated with belonging to the dominant Slavic group, characterized as White and Christian. Thus, despite the hardships they faced, Belarusians and Ukrainians played an important role in establishing Soviet state structures and were both victims and actors of Russian/Soviet colonialism.

It is the hope that future scholarship on Ukraine will further enrich analysis of this paradoxical status by dissociating policies of cultural and linguistic Russification that affected Ukrainian society and the latter's social and political role in co-managing the colonial project. To this we can add a third layer of Central Europe, which found themselves under Soviet influence for several decades without being part of the Soviet Union per se, and which also had to experience other forms of imperial domination (German, Austro-Hungarian) and then Nazi violence.

Another layer of critique centers on the implications of adopting a postcolonial stance, particularly in relation to the formulation of memory politics and nation-state ideology. As Serguei Oushakine has said in regard to the cases of Belarus and Kyrgyzstan, "the function of self-proclaimed postcoloniality is … a self-deprivation of any historical agency. Post-Soviet nationalist intellectuals encounter the insurmountable problems of the past, placing their nations retrospectively as the colonized, 'between Hitler and Stalin,' and therefore prefer to fashion themselves as passive and unarticulated objects of powerful historical forces."[261] Yet, for nations in the process of full nation-building, there is a distinct need for agency and a constructive framing of national identity because the adoption of a victimhood narrative can potentially weaken this imperative for agency and disempower efforts aimed at forging a positive national identity.

## Race, Racialism, Racism

An emerging area of research has been dedicated to exploring the applicability of the concept of race. The prevailing consensus has traditionally held that, unlike Western European empires, which propagated racial ideologies and institutionalized racial practices in their colonies, Russia exerted control and subjugation over non-Russian groups without relying on racial claims. Because Tsarist Russia was a traditionalist dynastic empire, the argument went, it did not need race to

---

[261] Gerasimov et al., "The Postimperial Meets the Postcolonial," 122; Serguei Oushakine, "Postcolonial Estrangements: Claiming a Space between Stalin and Hitler," in *Rites of Place: Public Commemoration in Russia and Eastern Europe*, ed. Julie Buckler and Emily D. Johnson (Northwestern University Press, 2013), 285–315; Serguei Oushakine, "The Colonial Scramble and Its Aftermath: Writing Public Histories of the Postcolonies of Socialism," *eSamizdat. Rivista di culture dei paesi slavi/Journal of Slavic Cultures* 14 (2021): 19–43.

naturalize relationships of domination and subjugation: color was never central to typologies of difference used in the Empire, with categories such as mother tongue, social estate, and religious confession being employed instead.

However, Marina Mogilner's pioneering works, *Homo Imperii: A History of Physical Anthropology in Russia* and *Jews, Race, and the Politics of Difference* challenge the prevailing notion that the Russian Empire was "nonclassical" and immune to racial theories.[262] Indeed, race as a language to construct groupness was widely used to code all types of differences from class to gender, from ethnic to civilizational. Equally, anti-imperial national movements also embraced race as a self-descriptive category to create a sense of belonging and to forge the notion of a modern nation. In the case of the Soviet Union, which actively cultivated a reputation for being colorblind and anti-racist, Eric D. Weitz argued that Stalin's large-scale deportations of certain groups during the 1930s and 1940s, including Chechens, Koreans, Cossacks, and others, constituted a form of "racial politics without the concept of race."[263]

Running parallel to this, Nathaniel Knight emphasized that ethnic rather than racial categories were predominant within the "vocabularies of difference" in the Russian Empire and the Soviet Union. He cautioned against overstating the similarities with other historical cases when discussing the prominence of race, as such an approach not only disregards the specificities of these cases but also risks obscuring the atrocities committed against racialized communities in Western empires.[264] Indeed, while it is true that some groups, especially those of Asian descent, may have experienced marginalization within the Russian Empire, they were nevertheless incorporated into intricate legal and semi-legal hierarchies, with each group being delineated on the map and assigned a distinct set of rights and duties – a trend that we see reflected in the Soviet ethno-federal system, too.[265]

---

[262] Marina Mogilner, *Homo Imperii: A History of Physical Anthropology in Russia* (University of Nebraska Press, 2013); Marina Mogilner, *Jews, Race, and the Politics of Difference: The Case of Vladimir Jabotinsky against the Russian Empire* (Indiana University Press, 2023).

[263] David Rainbow, "Introduction: Race as Ideology: An Approach," in *Ideologies of Race: Imperial Russia and the Soviet Union in Global Context*, ed. David Rainbow (McGill-Queen's University Press, 2019), 3–26, here p. 7; Eric D. Weitz, "Racial Politics without the Concept of Race: Reevaluating Soviet Ethnic and National Purges," *Slavic Review* 61, no. 1 (2002): 1–29. On this see also Eugene M. Avrutin, "The Most Hopeful Nation on Earth," in *Racism in Modern Russia: From the Romanovs to Putin* (Bloomsbury, 2022); Francine Hirsch, "Race without the Practice of Racial Politics," *Slavic Review* 61, no. 1 (2002): 30–43.

[264] Nathaniel Knight, "Vocabularies of Difference: Ethnicity and Race in Late Imperial and Early Soviet Russia," *Kritika* 13, no. 3 (Summer 2012): 667–83. For a critique of the resistance within the Russian and Soviet fields to characterizing the Soviet Union as a racial regime, see J. Otto Pohl, "Socialist Racism: Ethnic Cleansing and Racial Exclusion in the USSR and Israel," *Human Rights Review* (April–June 2006): 60–80.

[265] Viacheslav Morozov, "Post-Soviet Subalternity and the Dialectic of Race: Reflections on Tamar Koplatadze's Article," *Postcolonial Studies* 24, no. 1 (2021): 159–66.

In essence, constructivist approaches to the history of race have, at times, substituted one anachronistic premise (the idea that race is a primordial category of human difference) for another (the notion that race, as seen in Western Europe and its colonized regions, serves as the analytical norm). This might explain why understanding and comparing Russia's experiences with race have proven challenging. New approaches have invited the scholarly community to rethink the unacknowledged presence of race issue in sociological studies of Russia.[266]

## Religion as Decolonization

An area of research that has not yet been fully incorporated into the extensive body of scholarship on decolonial and postcolonial thinking in the context of Russia and its neighboring states is the role of religion, particularly Islam, in generating anticolonial discourse and advancing decolonial ideas.

The movement of Muslim modernists in Russia and Central Asia has been explored in the context of their contributions to the establishment of Bolshevik rule in the early Soviet Union. An ongoing debate persists regarding the nature of the Jadids, with scholars like Devin DeWeese arguing that they themselves were products of colonialism and hence inauthentic.[267] Adeeb Khalid, on the other hand, challenges an essentialist understanding of Islam in both Russian and Soviet contexts and calls for a critical reconsideration of the impact of imperial policies on Muslim subjectivities.[268] While some argue that Islam survived the Soviet Union, albeit in a transformed state,[269] contemporary scholarship in the region aims to "decolonize" Central Asian history and historiography by facilitating a proper "re-Islamization" of it.[270] This re-Islamization, often misconstrued in Western scholarship as religious radicalization, seeks to recover Indigenous cultures and values within their traditional religious and cultural contexts, which were marginalized by Russification and Sovietization.

The formulation of re-Islamization as a form of decolonization has encountered its own set of challenges. First of all, the claims of Islamic "Indigenousness" of the region encounter pushback from communities such as Tengrists and

---

[266] Marina Yusupova, "The Invisibility of Race in Sociological Research on Contemporary Russia: A Decolonial Intervention," *Slavic Review* 80, no. 2 (2021): 224–33.

[267] Devin DeWeese, "Review of Islam after Communism: Religion and Politics in Central Asia by Adeeb Khalid," *Journal of Islamic Studies* 19 (2007): 133–41.

[268] Adeeb Khalid, "Islam in Central Asia 30 Years after Independence: Debates, Controversies and the Critique of a Critique," *Central Asian Survey* 40, no. 4 (2021): 539–54.

[269] Tasar, *Soviet and Muslim*; for critique: Adeeb Khalid, "Review of *Soviet and Muslim* by Eren Tasar," *Slavic Review* 77, no. 4 (2018): 1035–37.

[270] R. Charles Weller, *"Pre-Islamic Survivals" in Muslim Central Asia: Tsarist, Soviet and Post-Soviet Ethnography in World Historical Perspective* (Springer Nature, 2023), 181.

Shamanists, who aim to recover the "pre-Islamic" past, thereby deconstructing the impact of Russian imperial institutions that viewed (and promoted) Islam as more advanced and civilized in comparison with supposedly primitive Shamanism and animism.

Furthermore, as "re-Islamization" has been coupled with the traditionalization of gender relations, the emancipatory promise of the decolonial Islamic scholarship has come under question in regard to gender. An analysis of the gender dynamics of Muslim communities in the Soviet project of modernization and colonialism requires further analysis, for the resurgence of conservative gender roles in post-Soviet Muslim-majority contexts may be attributed to the fact that Central Asian women, within the context of Soviet modernization, were not necessarily "modernized" in the first place.[271]

Lastly, it is important to note that while Islamic scholarship is inherently anticolonial, it does not necessarily align with Western de- or postcolonial perspectives. Islamic scholars often draw from Marxist-socialist sources in their critique of modern nation-states and nationalism, considering it a Western imperial imposition that contradicts Islamic norms, values, and ideals.[272]

## Exploring the Post-Soviet

Another notion that needs to be reconceptualized in line with the decoloniality frame is the notion of "post-Soviet." Initially, in a similar vein to "post-socialism," the term served merely as a temporal label denoting a supposed linear transition from socialism to various forms of democratization and market economy. However, over time, "post-Soviet" has emerged in scholarship as a critical perspective on the region's transformation. This critical stance encompassed an exploration of the socialist past, the potential for socialist futures, the dominance of neoliberal ideology imposed upon former socialist regions, and how knowledge was influenced by Cold War institutions.[273]

Can post-socialism be approached through the lens of postcolonial scholarship? An argument in favor of this approach is that post-socialist countries, much like their postcolonial counterparts, underwent heightened national

---

[271] Adrienne Edgar, "Bolshevism, Patriarchy, and the Nation: The Soviet 'Emancipation' of Muslim Women in Pan-Islamic Perspective," *Slavic Review* 65, no. 2 (2006): 252–72; Adeeb Khalid, "Locating the (Post-)Colonial in Soviet History," *Central Asian Survey* 26, no. 4 (2007): 471.

[272] E.g., Salman Sayyid, *Recalling the Caliphate: Decolonization and World Order* (Hurst Publishers, 2022).

[273] Sharad Chari and Katherine Verdery, "Thinking between the Posts: Postcolonialism, Postsocialism, and Ethnography after the Cold War," *Comparative Studies in Society and History* 51, no. 1 (2009): 10–11.

consciousness during socio-political transformations. Both share a sense of incomplete rupture from cultural and economic ties that linked peripheries to metropoles.[274] However, extending postcolonial theory to the point where post-socialism is seen merely as a variant of postcolonialism represents an oversimplification of the specificities of each context.[275] Notably, nationalisms in post-socialist states often predated the emergence of state-socialist regimes. Consequently, the anti-Russian sentiments observed in post-Soviet European countries differ significantly from the complex identity struggles of postcolonial subjects with their former colonizers.[276]

Moreover, for Central and Eastern countries such as the Baltic states and Ukraine, the political realities of wanting to join or having joined the European Union have introduced new complexities to the way in which academia frames the notion of national belonging.[277] In such a context, the term "post-Soviet" expresses the challenge of capturing what remains or not of the Soviet experience. What commonality, which divergences, which dynamics? Is "regionness" a useful concept for social scientists to understand the ongoing changes? When do we think the post-Soviet societies will stop being "post-Soviet," and is there a *post*-post-Sovietism? What criteria should be used to determine the advent of this post-post-Sovietism: changes of regime, generation replacement, cultural changes, nationhood framing? With Russia's full-scale invasion of Ukraine, academic institutions have been invited to rethink their use of the terms "Eurasia" and "post-Soviet" and to reconceptualize the relationship to both "Europe" and "Asia" – both of which are constructed nations that carry complex and multifaceted meanings.

## Global Coloniality and Academic Ghettoization

Postcolonial theory also poses a challenge to scholars of post-socialism, as it can create a dependence on what seems to be a Southern scholarly endeavor but ultimately reflects the continued hegemony of the North Atlantic in academia.[278] In such a context, a fruitful area of research has involved examining Russia and its neighboring countries within the framework of global

---

274 Radim Hladík, "A Theory's Travelogue: Post-Colonial Theory in Post-Socialist Space," *Teorie Vědy/Theory of Science* 33, no. 4 (2011): 575.

275 Moore, "Is the Post- in Postcolonial the Post- in Post-Soviet?"

276 Hladík, "A Theory's Travelogue," 576.

277 E.g., Dorota Kołodziejczyk and Siegfried Huigen, eds, *East Central Europe between the Colonial and the Postcolonial in the Twentieth Century* (Springer International Publishing, 2023); Janusz Korek, ed., *From Sovietology to Postcoloniality: Poland and Ukraine from a Postcolonial Perspective* (Södertörns högskola, 2007); Violeta Kelertas, ed., *Baltic Postcolonialism* (Rodopi, 2006); Clare Cavanagh, "Postcolonial Poland," *Common Knowledge* 10, no. 1 (2004): 82–92.

278 Hladík, "A Theory's Travelogue," 589.

coloniality.[279] While colonialism refers to a historical phenomenon, coloniality addresses its present-day implications. The decolonial approach focuses not on the historical account of (neo)colonialist strategies but rather on the enduring ontological, epistemic, and axiological imprints that persist long after colonialism has faded.

In line with this, scholarship from the region often complains about Western – and more specifically US (or at least English-speaking) – social science hegemony. In the context of global inequalities – in economic terms, and not unrelated to them, in terms of knowledge production – as Eszter Kováts framed it, "how do concepts and causes that are intended to be emancipatory fall into the trap of ignoring local contexts and follow a colonial or imperial logic, communicated through channels of power (political elites, institutions, funding, media, academia)?"[280] Theories from the so-called Global South, which often, in this case, includes Eurasian or post-Soviet scholarship, can contribute to a better understanding of developments in the West as much as Western-produced works. To put it another way, non-Western scholarship claims the right to universalism too and there is and will be resistance "to new global hegemonic theories of postcoloniality that are not 'forged' in local experience and are not rooted in the local intellectual tradition."[281]

## Moving Forward

There are several strategies for decolonizing the field.[282] First and foremost, this can be achieved by creating more research opportunities focused on other societies within the region, utilizing perspectives and frameworks that do not derive from the tsarist/Soviet context. As described earlier in this section, moving beyond the "Post-Soviet" can offer new lenses for inquiry. For example, researchers could explore Central Asia through its connections with the Middle Eastern and Chinese worlds, a direction that Central Asian scholarship has been pursuing since the 2000s, as a means to counterbalance a Russia-centered analysis.

Second, there is a need to reconsider the ethnocentric lens through which Russia is often viewed, which has led to the neglect of ethnic minorities in research. The general Western lack of knowledge of Russia's national languages and the marginalization of identity politics, seen as a "sub-area" that cannot explain Russia's general features, have left entire spaces understudied. This

---

[279] Madina Tlostanova and Walter Mignolo, "Global Coloniality and the Decolonial Option," *Kult* 6 (2009): 130–47.

[280] Eszter Kováts, "Introduction," in *Culture Wars in Europe*, ed. Eszter Kováts (Illiberalism Studies Program, IERES GWU, 2023), ii.

[281] Gorshenina, "Orientalism," 223.

[282] Marlene Laruelle, "Russian Studies' Moment of Self-Reflection," *Russian Analytical Digest* 293 (March 3, 2023): 2–3.

"blank spot" is not only an issue in the West. Indeed, as Vitaly Chernetsky notes throughout the 1990s, Russian academics largely ignored postcolonial debates, and, although one of the significant accomplishments of postcolonial studies in the West has been to raise awareness in former imperial metropoles about their historical responsibilities to their former colonies, the situation concerning Russia and its Soviet past has remained complex.[283]

Third, and related, it is important to move away from a Moscow-centric vision of Russia, where the capital city and its more liberal residents can overshadow the diverse and nuanced perspectives found in the regions. Grassroots research on provincial Russia can tells us as much, if not more, about the country. Again, this permeates both Western and Russian scholarship; scholars from Russia's central institutions in Moscow and Saint Petersburg have little interest in their regional colleagues, who are relegated to conducting "regional studies." Thus, both Western and Russian scholarship should pay more attention to regional colleagues and their work, recognizing that regional studies are just as legitimate and important as research from central institutions.[284] This extends to critically reevaluating existing historiographies, uncovering their biases and instrumentalization by political actors, as well as further evaluating how certain historiographies become transplanted or influence scholarship across time and space.[285] This, inevitably, requires further reflection on the pedagogical approaches to teaching about Russia.

The fourth move forward relates to the field's geographical siloing and power hierarchy. The dominance of English-language literature means that other literatures – such as those written in other European languages, in languages of former Soviet republics, of Russia's ethnic minorities or in Russian – have hitherto been overlooked or ignored altogether. This trend is particularly visible in political science, and less so in the humanities. This raises another series of questions regarding the lack of cross-disciplinarity in political science. The growth of experimental social science – stressing the need for causal identification study designs and drawing heavily upon survey data – has been "both a curse and a blessing for Russian studies."[286] While, on the one hand, this led to a proliferation of new social science research after the Cold War,[287] with

---

[283] Vitaly Chernetsky, "On Some Post-Soviet Postcolonialisms," *PMLA* 121, no. 3 (2006): 833–36.

[284] For example, see Chimiza Lamazhaa, "Russian Regional Science in an Asymmetric System," The Russia Program at GW, September 2023, https://therussiaprogram.org/regional_science.

[285] Susan Smith-Peter and Sean Pollock, "How the Field Was Colonized: Russian History's Ukrainian Blind Spot," *Russian History* 50, no. 3–4 (2024): 145–56.

[286] Alexander Libman, "Credibility Revolution and the Future of Russian Studies," *Post-Soviet Affairs* 39, no. 1–2 (March 4, 2023): 60–69, here p. 60.

[287] Scott Gehlbach and Edmund Malesky, 'The Grand Experiment That Wasn't? New Institutional Economics and the Postcommunist Experience', in *Institutions, Property Rights, and Economic Growth: The Legacy of Douglass North*, ed. Sebastián Galiani and Itai Sened (Cambridge University Press, 2014), 225.

Russia-focused scholars able to publish Russia-focused studies in top social science journals, on the other hand such disciplinary and methodological siloing came at the expense of interactions with history, cultural anthropology, sociology, or geography, leaving many dynamics and patterns in Russian society and political development understudied. Here, too, the segregation is largely internal to the "Western" and especially Anglophone realm: Russian-language publications display much deeper cross-disciplinary approaches.

Last but not least, power hierarchies occur not only between Russia/Russians and neighboring countries/ethnic minorities within Russia but are also intimately linked to Western knowledge production dominance. The West is presented as the only mirror of Russia, representing a glaring exclusion of views from non-Western perspectives. Scholars from countries neighboring Russia have increasingly called for their agency to be recognized in interpreting Russia on the basis of their own experiences. Scholars from the Global South, too, look at Russia and at the West through their own prisms and experiences, including a vivid postcolonial approach, which often remains marginalized.

## Conclusion

The debate on decolonizing Russia, as well as the field of Russian studies, draws on the assumption of Russia being an empire. From our short analysis in this study for the *Elements* series, several conclusions can be drawn. The first is that, contrary to nationalism studies, which have deconstructed the notions of nation and nation-state to explore identity-belonging and how polities are built, and the huge and vibrant field of postcolonial studies, there does not really exist an "empire studies" subfield – with the exception, in the Russian case, of the journal *Ab Imperio* – that would deconstruct what it means to be an empire. The term "empire" has therefore remained mostly used as a negative label to denounce a country seen as nationalist, authoritarian, and aggressive, but has not been articulated regarding issues related to the fluidity and hybridity of identities, their situational nature, and the complex symbolic hierarchies of belonging to a multinational polity.

The second conclusion is that if the imperial prism is indeed meaningful to comprehend many elements of the evolution of Russia and of its peoples, it cannot be the only lens of study. Too often, for instance, projecting Russia's imperialism becomes intertwined with the nature of today's political regime, without demonstrating the causality between being imperial and being authoritarian. When the Kremlin is repressing grassroots civil society in ethnic regions, is that a feature of authoritarianism, applied across all regions of the country, or a feature of imperialism, applied in a specific way to curb ethnic belonging? We are still missing works tackling the comparison between ethnic republics and Russian regions to comprehend the top–down logic of repression and how local actors deal with it. The imperial lens is thus relevant, but it is just one among many other conceptual toolkits one can use to comprehend the Russian state and Russian society.

One also needs to keep granularity in mind and be careful to avoid a reading that is too uniform. Historical periodization matters, as Russia's imperial nature has expressed itself differently across time. Spatial realities matter too, as the different nations (which used to be before or continue be part of the Russian-centric state formations) have experienced different ways of being integrated, co-opted, promoted, and repressed – sometimes simultaneously. Being an ethnic minority in Russia's large and multinational metropoles, with newcomers from all over the country and abroad, differs greatly from being an ethnic minority in a rural, isolated place and on its own natives' lands. The segregated nature of ethnicity in Russia, with clearly identifiable ethnic regions (North Caucasus and Volga-Urals in particular), has evolved dramatically since the 2000s, with the mass departure of young people from small-town ethnic minority backgrounds toward Russia's big metropoles. The question of intersectionality appears, then, a critical issue to take into consideration: In everyday life, the dichotomy between urbans and rurals, middle classes and impoverished segments of the population is often more important than between being Russian or belonging to an ethnic minority.

Our third conclusion is that there is a tendency in Western analyses to look at Russia's past imperial/colonial practices without recontextualizing them: On many aspects, the Russian elites articulated an imperial/colonial vision that was not so different from their Western counterparts, and the Soviet experience should be read through its Europeanness too. Both tsarist and Soviet Russia shared with the West a similar set of beliefs such as a universalistic civilizing mission, economic and societal modernization, and subjugation of the natural environment, but implemented them differently both for contingent reasons, such as the continental scope of the Russian Empire versus Western overseas empires and a socialist interpretation of modernity versus a capitalist one. The narratives otherizing Russia as representing an absolute, essentialist, opposition to Western values then project retroactively over time the current ideological conflict, but conveniently forget that the West has been itself imperial, colonial, retrograde, etc. – and some would say continues to be neo-imperial, neocolonial, and illiberal in some of its features.

Comparative research is therefore needed to better capture what makes the Russian imperial experience specific and which features are shared with other imperial polities. We are still missing a whole range of historical works comparing, for instance, the US colonization of its territory and Russia's conquest of

Siberia, the experiences of Indigenous nations on both sides, and some more audacious works to be done on racial experiences in the USA and in Russia, or on the postcolonial features of labor migration from the Middle East to Europe, and from Central Asia and the Caucasus to Russia. On the more contemporary period, Russia's illiberal regime would also benefit from more in-depth comparisons with, for instance, the Chinese, Turkish, Egyptian, Algerian, or Iranian cases, among many others.

It is therefore time to de-Westernize our analysis of Russia and take into consideration other examples of comparison, such as China or India (one could add Brazil, Indonesia, etc.), which are, too, political entities with multinational diversity and tensions between center and peripheries. This non-Euro-centric vision of Russia would contribute to normalizing (which does not mean justifying), and not exceptionalizing, Russia's experience of the multinational and how it articulates with a narrative on sovereignty – here too, a central notion for many countries of the Global South.

Part of the decolonialization of our own analysis is also to remember power hierarchy inside the knowledge production chain and the need to analyze Russia by giving more prominence to unheard voices. This means also recognizing that grassroots decolonial claims may not come under a liberal framework, but emerge from non-liberal, sometimes anti-liberal, assumptions. The dichotomy is not between being liberal versus being imperial – which tends to be the way Western media and punditry comments on Russia's current war against Ukraine. Liberalism has long been imperial, too, and decolonization may also mean, in some contexts, being anti- or non-liberal.

Our original motivation in writing this volume in the Elements series was to provide a scholarly perspective on many of the conversations taking place among academic circles, the media, and policymakers on the need to "decolonize" Russia in the wake of its full-scale invasion of Ukraine in February 2022. As scholars, we felt best placed to contribute to these conversations by providing analysis, contextualization, and, where necessary, critique. It remains to be seen how such debates will evolve in the coming months and years; if anything, this Element cautions us to be intellectually modest in terms of what we can and cannot predict.

However, "decolonization" has visibly entered a broader semantic space; it has articulated and accentuated existing cleavages and grievances present before 2022, been wielded in new contexts and by different actors for various ends, and has even entered into narratives used by the Kremlin at home and abroad. As we have suggested in this Element, much will depend upon how "decolonization" comes to be perceived by individuals and groups themselves, their goals and constraints, and the broader political context of the Russian regime. But these are debates worth paying attention to.

# Acknowledgements

We wish to thank the editors of the Element series, Mark Edele and Rebecca Friedman, for their support of the project. We are also grateful to Chris Ellison for helpful editing, as well as to the various friends and colleagues who provided feedback on the manuscript at various stages, including the anonymous reviewers, Jesko Schmoller, Sergei, and Masha.